# CRADOCK
## *on*
# SHOTGUNS

# CRADOCK

*on* SHOTGUNS

*Chris Cradock*

B.T.Batsford Ltd, London

ISBN 0 7134 5965 4 (cased)

Typeset by Keyspools Ltd, Golborne, Lancs
and printed in Great Britain
by The Bath Press, Bath
for the publishers
B.T.Batsford Ltd
4 Fitzhardinge Street
London W1H 0AH

# Contents

# Foreword

For many years there has been a need for a definitive up-to-date book covering all aspects of shotguns and their use. To anyone with any knowledge of the field there could only be one person to write such a book, and that is Chris Cradock.

There can be absolutely no dispute that Chris is the doyen of modern shotgun writers with a fund of practical and theoretical knowledge that has taken a lifetime of enthusiasm and interest to acquire.

Chris has an inimitable personality which has always been integral to his willingness and ability to communicate his knowledge. As one of many who have benefited from his help over the years I can only be thankful that he has finally brought all his knowledge together in one master work.

*Cradock on Shotguns* is sure to find a place on every shooting enthusiast's bookshelf and will prove invaluable to many for its bibliography alone. The sheer scope of this book, covering everything from the technicalities of guns and their design to the niceties of shooting style and behaviour, makes it unique. It is full of sound common sense, too, and will serve as an instruction manual, an entertainment and a reference book for many years to come.

It is a fine testament to a life spent – misspent Chris might say – in shooting.

John Fletcher

# Preface

This book is based on experience gained from handling, stripping down, reassembling, and shooting guns for the past sixty years and more, during which time I have shot most types of shotgun from flintlock to the modern superb examples of the gun maker's art obtainable as singles, side by sides, over and under, semi-automatic, and pump guns.

Shooting friends with extensive libraries of shooting books have been most kind and for most of my lifetime I have had access to the majority of shooting books produced since 1785. I have read the *Shooting Times* and *The Field* for as long as I can remember, always attempting to distil theory from the written word and then prove such theories in practice before accepting them as gospel. Theories which have not worked out in practice have been discarded. Friends in gun making both in this country and abroad have been more than generous in showing me the best of gun making, most of those in the trade are enthusiasts and spare no effort to produce the goods, also to show the layman the how and the why. This regardless of how busy they have been. Nothing has been too much trouble.

For many years I have been technical advisor to the *Shooting Magazine* and worked briefly as gun editor for *Shooting Times*, for whom readers' shooting queries were a major feature. Tests on guns, cartridges and equipment for these magazines have provided more experience. I have written several articles for *Eley Shooters Diary*, *The Field*, *Insight* and the CPSA house magazine *Pull*. Thousands of queries have been received and answered from readers of the above magazines all over the world.

My coaching experience has been acquired by running a shooting school, at the Game Fair, as the first CPSA National Coach and Safety Officer. In addition, trips to the United States to advise on new Sporting Clay Target layouts have helped to solve many shooting problems. I have learned from this and the experience of many others that the real problem is usually the gun operator. Any man or woman can buy or acquire the finest equipment and cartridges, have a 'best' gun specially fitted and made. All this is fine but without 100 per cent motivation and willingness to serve a full apprenticeship, that man or woman will never achieve his or her true and full potential. This shooting apprenticeship requires hours of training. Constant practice in gun handling and shooting shows how owner and gun can operate harmoniously most of the time.

One has only to watch an expert stocker fitting a stock to a shotgun action and observe over many hours of careful painstaking work how that blank is transformed into an integral part of the finished gun. Everything blends, the fit of wood to metal is perfect. The ideal of any shooting person should be to acquire the same blending of muscular and mental harmony between owner and tool, this tool being the shotgun.

This expertise does not come by chance or by luck. It has to be worked for by hours of constant handling and training until eventually he or she acquires 'muscle memory'. Until the owner can do this he or she will never scale the heights and produce a performance to equal that of the gun and cartridge. A good coach can teach anyone with normal coordination to hit any clay target or live quarry in range. Only the shooter can produce that intestinal fortitude which strings the hits together into peak performances.

There are no easy targets: targets and live quarry must be taken and shot at one at a time. That particular target must be regarded as *the one* on which he or she must wholly concentrate. To watch others' scores or performances and try and work out how many targets are required for success is a waste of time and energy. All the shooter has to do is to keep on breaking targets. If he or she does this no-one can beat the straight so produced. They can only tie. The same goes for live quarry shooting. All must be well aware of their own capabilities. They must have acquired confidence in themselves, their guns and ammunition. Then, with the correct technique, they should fear no-one, producing good performances most of the time. When at odd times the magic departs, and it will, the remedy is back to the shooting school. There a session with one's favourite coach will provide the correct answer and re-awaken motivation. Post-mortems in the bar that evening by laymen or chance acquaintances will only produce guesstimates, gimmicks and quack remedies, none of which can work except by chance.

As explained elsewhere, the amount of shooting know-how, so readily available these days, is greater than ever. The young especially have everything going for them. The majority of shooting coaches love coaching the young entry, who can usually be expected to be 100 per cent on the side of their coach, they will listen and try to do what the coach suggests. Moreover the young entry has no bad habits to unlearn and discard. The mature shot who comes belatedly to a shooting school is a different problem. Life has taught these people to believe little of what they are told until they are 'shown', resulting in unbelievers at worst, or unwilling believers at best. At first they are usually mediocre performers and although very willing to pay any amount of money to acquire a superb 'best' fitted gun they are often unwilling to work on learning how to handle their gun to its best advantage. Even more disheartening are those who for no obvious reason believe they are really 'natural shots', and it should therefore follow that the spending of much money on a fitted gun will provide its owner with the complete answer for instant success. The honest approach to such people is to explain these problems in detail, then suggest that they change their approach or change their sport. Being mostly hard-headed business people they are used to evaluating propositions and will see the common sense and wisdom of the coach's advice.

Some of the material in these pages has appeared in the above journals, especially *Shooting Magazine* and *Shooting Times*. Although all contained here has been rewritten, the basics are still as they were and always have been. My thanks go to the editors of the magazines concerned for permission to use my original articles in a revamped form; to those kind people at the CPSA, the Proof houses, the Game Conservancy and BASC; to all in the gun and cartridge trade, at shooting schools and clay clubs (there are so many, it is not possible to mention all by name). To my many other friends, and I have never been refused help by anyone, I offer my sincere thanks. I hope this book will be regarded as a small tribute to all friends of the gun and harmonious shooting technique.

I have referred to the shooter as 'he' for simplicity of style. Of course this book is addressed to the ladies also.

C.D. Cradock.

*'This gun is empty'* (courtesy N. Penn, Pennsport S.G.)

# 1
# Gun Safety

THIS aspect of shooting is *most important*: the subject deserves a book, not just a chapter. Therefore gun safety is given pride of place in this book. If a lifetime of handling and observing others handling guns has taught me anything at all, it is that most people are happy when they are in the company of someone who handles his safely. They are most unhappy when in the company of those who do not. It is a fact that 'shooting is a sport of responsibility'. Another dictum which should never be forgotten is, 'Safety, wasted precautions are never regretted'.

## A Deadly Weapon

The shotgun is an instrument designed for killing, which was the reason it came into being. Centuries of development have resulted in a frighteningly efficient and effective weapon. A surgeon friend who knows what he is talking about likens the destructive powers of a charge of shot from a gun to that of a hand grenade. Humans make mistakes. My own concern has always been that I may do something stupid. At least twice in my lifetime I have been guilty of unsafe gun handling. Although this was many years ago, and no harm came to anyone the memory burns me still.

## Constant Vigilance

Those handling guns must practise constant vigilance. It will not do to 'think' a gun is empty. The prime example of the 'seen to be safe' gun handlers are gun shop workers. No matter how many times they take a gun from the racks, they always open it to see it is empty; turning the open gun to the customer they say 'this gun is empty'. Maybe minutes before they opened the same gun to check before returning it to the rack. They treat all guns as loaded until visually proved to be empty and safe. So no matter, and as standard routine, the procedure is gone through again and again and again. The coach before handing any gun to anyone, always opens that gun to show that it is empty. When gun fitting he then closes it, hands it to the client and with the words 'I know the gun is empty', asks his client to point it at the coach's finger to check for master eye, gun fit or whatever.

Any shotgun is a piece of machinery. No piece of mechanism can be relied upon to be 100 per cent free from wear, tear, faults – latent or developed, and/or breakages. One of the greatest gun designers, John M. Browning, remarked with feeling, 'what man makes – man breaks'.

## SAFETY CATCHES

### Automatic Safety Catches

There are really no such things. An automatic safety catch is simply a mechanical contrivance which is moved to 'safe' when the gun action is opened. Then, although the safety thumb piece shows 'safe' all that safety catch does is to mechanically block the trigger movement. It does not prevent sear noses from being jarred out of their bents and the tumblers being released. It is true that sear noses and bents as turned out by good gun makers are mated together as a good fit and give little trouble but even the best sear noses have been and can be jarred out of their bents. When this happens if that gun is loaded the release of the tumbler will cause it to fire. Few safety catches mechanically hold the sear noses in their bents thereby blocking the sear release.

### Manual Safety Catches

These stay where they are put by the gun owner. When the gun is opened the safety catch still stays in the same position as when set by the owner. When the safety slide is moved to show 'safe' it should not be possible to move the trigger and release the sear. If the slide is moved to 'fire' the trigger can be pulled and the sear released. The same principle applies that normally only the triggers are mechanically restrained and sears can still be jarred out of bents.

Therefore shooting etiquette requires that all guns be carried open and empty when and wherever possible. Muzzle awareness is cultivated by all who handle guns. As a result no closed gun will ever have its muzzles pointed at anything the owner does not wish to kill. Even when a closed gun is in a gun slip or full-length sleeve cover the gun and cover is never carried at the trail, experience having proved that no closed gun can ever safely be regarded as being unloaded.

## Other Safety Catch Problems

Guns with manual safety catches and heavy single trigger assemblies: if the trigger assembly is very heavy and the gun has the safety slide on fire and if there are no mechanical means of moving the sear nose well out of bent, it may be possible by slamming the gun shut to jar the sear or sears out of bent(s). If that gun has just been loaded it will then fire when so slammed shut.

## SAFE GUN HANDLING

It is true that such premature firing may be due to unsafe gun handling; but if that gun was also being held with the muzzles pointed in an unsafe direction the end result of slamming a loaded gun shut when so held can be just as deadly. These are facts and justify the prudent gun owner's belief that each and every one must cultivate 100 per cent awareness of one's muzzle and gun point at all times. To the best of my knowledge no-one has ever been killed by an open and seen-to-be-empty gun. Gun accidents are caused by closed and loaded guns pointing in an unsafe manner.

It is sad that most people whether inexperienced or not believe they are 'safe gun handlers'. Even the most inexperienced gun owner seems to resent being shown the basics of safe gun handling by an expert. This is a dangerous and foolhardy attitude. These basic safety-handling skills can only be acquired by hours of gun handling practice in the presence of a competent coach.

It is preferable to begin with snap caps. A mistake with snap caps only produces a click as the tumbler falls. A mistake with a loaded cartridge may result in tragedy. To read a book such as this is just not good enough. All gun owners and shooters *must* do their 'practical'. Theory is fine, but there is *no* substitute for practical experience gained under the watchful eyes of an expert. Even when fully taught he or she must still act safely at all times. Everyone must be their own safety officers, no responsibility can be taken by this writer. The presence of an expert coach when the tyro begins his gun handling is a must. The safe and quiet confines of a shooting school or the practice stand at a clay club is the place to cultivate these good and safe gun handling habits by any beginner of whatever age. Being inexperienced such clients have no bad habits to

*A gun carried open can be seen to be empty*

unlearn or discard. They are 100 per cent on the side of the coach, accept his teaching and do what they are told. This course of instruction with a good coach should produce safe and competent shots – most welcome at a clay club or shooting field.

## Behaviour at the Clay Club

Here the pressures to conform are greater than when shooting live quarry. Usually many more experienced shots will be standing near and watching closely for errors by the novice. The shooting stands will or should be safely positioned. The fallout area for the shot pellets should be devoid of humans or other forms of life. The referee, safety officers and the committee know the form and will quietly try to prevent any unsafe gun handling. This provides a safety net for someone shooting say DTL in an irresponsible manner. This before a referee or safety officer could prevent it happening. Because of this fact, most gun clubs rightly will not allow the novice to shoot in a squad until he knows how to behave safely. Gun clubs these days have their club coaches who will be pleased to instruct and also advise when they believe a novice is ready to join a squad and shoot for real as opposed to shooting at a quiet coaching trap stand away from the rest of the club shooting activities. All of which is right and proper.

## Safe Behaviour when Shooting Live Quarry

It is the responsibility of the shooter not to shoot where he cannot see. When standing at a shooting peg, the prudent sportsman or woman always makes certain he or she knows exactly where stops, beaters, other guns, and pickers up are positioned. If there is any doubt on such matters the prudent owner will refrain from firing. To take low shots into or just over bushes, to shoot into woods, etc. is forbidden. The safe rule is 'if in doubt don't shoot'.

## TO SUM UP

All guns can kill. It is essential that owners keep this fundamental fact in their mind and act accordingly at all times. Those who are taking up live quarry shooting, even after a full shooting school course of instruction, should always go to a few live shoots with a friend as an observer. This will allow one's friend to explain the correct form. All guns should be periodically checked and kept in safe shootable in-proof conditions at all times. The cartridges must be compatible. Check barrels for obstructions before loading live cartridges. If you hear an odd sound as you fire a cartridge, always blow down the barrel of the opened gun. Then visually check by looking down the barrels for obstructions. A famous coach used to advise as follows: 'The sportsman or woman who does not visually check by looking down the barrels from the breech after an odd sounding shot doesn't need a loader, he or she needs a nurse maid.'

The owner must play his part by safe gun handling at all times. Wherever possible guns must be carried open and empty. There are those who claim the carrying of an open gun stresses the knuckle joint. Robert Churchill was a well-known gun maker and told me half a century ago that good guns could be carried open and empty without suffering any harm. The well-known poem printed in *Eley Shooters Diary* should be known by heart; it must also be acted upon and acted upon. So should be the CPSA's ten commandments for safe shooting. Muzzle awareness must be cultivated and practised until it is as natural as breathing. All closed guns should be treated as loaded and with the greatest suspicion. Guns and cartridges should be kept well away and safely secure from inexperienced persons, or the criminal element. Shooting is indeed a sport of responsibility and we all *must* be our own safety officers.

Advice for those parents or guardians who are non shooters and are being badgered by their offspring to let said offspring take up shooting: this is the normal enthusiasm of the young brave since time immemorial. There are many far more dangerous pursuits to take up than shooting. It is unrealistic to forbid young Johnny to shoot. At the first opportunity he will slip off with some like-minded and usually older friend. That way can lie tragedy. Far better to grasp the nettle, take the young entry to a local gun shop, and ask the manager to explain the pros and cons of safe gun ownership. Decide how much money is available for a suitable fitted gun. Arrange to have a trial shoot at a local school, after which some will decide the sport is not for them. Others will be sold on the idea and wish to take up clay shooting. Enquiries can be made at a local club. This can be visited and the club safety officer or coach will explain what is required by and from members. He or she will also advise on correct clothing, head gear, shooting glasses, and hearing protection. As indeed will the local gun shop. The chosen clay club should be affiliated to the CPSA. There any youngster will be well received and helped in every way. Very often the parent also becomes interested and also takes up the sport. The essential criteria are that the young are taught safe and responsible gun handling by a pro right from the word go. Youngsters thus taught are a pleasure both to meet and to shoot with, growing in stature and becoming increasingly responsible in their behaviour as their shooting improves. Compare these fortunates with the young who are repressed or prevented from being taught to handle a gun safely. They usually break out eventually and then are greatly at risk, often a menace to themselves and any living thing unfortunate enough to be within pellet fallout distance.

All sportsmen and women should be holders of a valid shotgun certificate. They should also be insured against third party claims. Paid up members of BASC or the CPSA are so covered.

# 2
# The Modern Shotgun

PRESENT day shotguns are the result of many years' development, the product of countless craftsmen and women who have spent their lives translating the wishes of the shooting fraternity into guns which are superb tools. They are available in all grades. Owners who take the trouble to learn the efficient handling of these tools soon realize their good fortune, also the pleasure and privilege of owning and shooting such an excellent tool or weapon. A well-fitted and handled gun seems to be an extension of its owner's front hand and arm, eagerly pointing to the exact spot where its owner is looking.

This is true whether the gun is single barrel, double barrel, of side by side, or over and under construction. Furthermore a 'best' gun is always a best gun regardless of its type. Correctly handled, fuelled, and maintained such guns are a joy to own and shoot not only for the lifetime of their original fortunate owners but also for their descendants. Here are brief details of the guns currently on sale.

## 1 SINGLE BARREL SINGLE SHOTGUN

### Boxlock Break Open Action Design

Available in all qualities. At the lower end of the price range these singles are popular as first guns for the novice. May be hammer or hammerless,

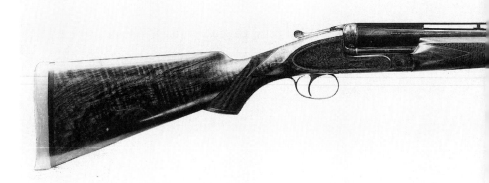

*Purdey 'best' single barrel sidelock hammerless ejector trap gun*

*Remington pump gun*

with automatic ejection whether or not the cartridge has been fired. The barrel hinges downwards when the gun is opened.

## Martini Action Falling Block Gun

The Greener G.P. Martini is a popular example. The action and ejector is easily opened and closed by an underlever. Simple, strong, and durable. In expert hands has been loaded and fired at 18 shots per minute.

## Best Quality Single Barrel Single Shotgun

Available with sidelock or boxlock ejector actions. Favoured by American trap shooters. Precision tools providing years of trouble free service.

## 2 Single Barrel Pump Gun

These single-barrelled guns have hand operated slide or pump actions. The shooter trombones or pumps the action backwards and forwards to eject the fired case and load a live round from the magazine into the

*Beretta semi-automatic gun*

barrel chamber. An expert can fire and empty a fully loaded pump gun more quickly than he can a semi-automatic shotgun. Pump guns are usually machine made, medium-priced and more popular on the Continent and in America than in Great Britain. Should steel shot become mandatory for some forms of live quarry shooting the pump and the semi-automatic guns can be expected to become more popular, their single barrels having thicker walls which may allow the owner to fire steel shot cartridges without damage.

## 3 Single Barrel Semi-automatic Gun

First choice of many modern wildfowlers, rough, and clay target shooters. Can be inertia, gas or recoil operated. Medium-priced examples of these guns, correctly maintained, are usually trouble free, inexpensive, versatile with good performances. Obtainable in many grades. Some are more choosey regarding ammunition than others.

**Beretta** o/u **boxlock hammerless ejector gun**

**W.&C. Scott** s/s **boxlock hammerless ejector gun**

## 4 Side by Side Guns

*Boxlock Hammerless Guns*

Modern examples are usually based on Anson and Deeley design, with double or single selective triggers. With manual live cartridge or fired cartridge case extraction or with selective ejectors.

The sportsman with enough time and money can buy a side by side boxlock hammerless ejector gun of Anson and Deeley design to almost any specification, these boxlock actions being still manufactured in many parts of the world. They give little trouble, are efficient, long wearing and can be bought in all grades up to 'best'.

## Sidelock Hammerless Ejector Guns

Also available in all grades to almost any specification. 'Best' guns of this type represent the pinnacle of gun making. Best materials, best workmanship, they are hand fitted and assembled by means of the smoke lamp. Some may have been allowed to rust out. Correctly maintained and fuelled these guns are seemingly everlasting. One example fired over a million cartridges with approximately one thousandth of an inch wear in the barrel internal diameter.

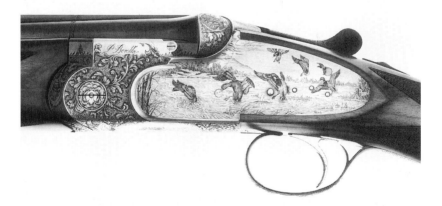

*Beretta o/u sidelock hammerless ejector gun*

## 5 Over and Under Gun

Described as 'superposed' in America. This barrel construction is not new; muzzle loaders were available a hundred years ago with stacked barrels. Modern guns are available in most grades and designs. As boxlock, with or without trigger plate action, sidelock, with selective ejectors and double trigger, single triggers or single selective triggers. Safeties either manual or automatic. Top ribs can be solid, raised, ramped, ventilated, of various widths and anti-glare surfaces. Barrel lengths are from 24–32 in, chokes interchangeable or integral.

Modern gun prices are competitive; a good working gun can cost a few hundred pounds, a 'best' gun costs thousands and is worth every penny. Given enough time 'best' guns whether side by side or over and under can be produced to any safe specification and to fit the purchaser.

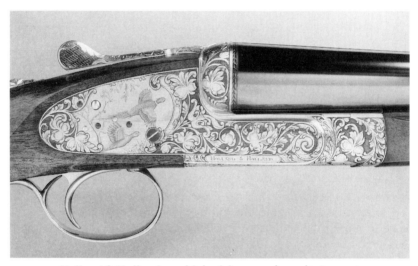

*Holland & Holland s/s sidelock hammerless ejector gun*

# 3
# Buying a Gun

## OBTAINING VALUE FOR MONEY

THE manufacture, importing, and/or selling of shotguns, cartridges and accessories is a highly competitive business. The economics of the market place ensure no business will survive for long unless the goods for sale are priced competitively and the quality of goods and after-sales services give full value. A wise buyer will select an established gun shop – if possible locally – and rely on their integrity. A knowledgeable purchaser should be able to obtain good value for money regardless of whether the gun purchased is new or secondhand.

The tyro cannot know the questions to ask or the correct answers and is most at risk. Guns for sale privately may be bargains or over priced; they may also be death-traps. The private seller may be a man of straw, and, in the case of obtaining one's money back or other recompense, for instance for an out-of-proof gun, there may be no money available. Therefore the tyro should take as first choice an established gun shop. All buyers must first decide for what purpose the gun will be used, the probable number of cartridges per annum it will fire and how much money they wish to spend. Then he should visit the local gun shop on a fact-finding mission, allowing plenty of time. Hundreds, even thousands of pounds may be spent. Unless the gun shop manager is in possession of the above facts he cannot advise. It also makes sense to insist on having a trial shoot with the help of a try-gun at a shooting school to check gun fit and assess the cost of any alterations to stock balance, choking, trigger pulls, etc., which may be advisable.

**Perazzi stock measuring machine** (Leslie Hewett)

## Gun Fitting

Attempts at gun fitting in the gun shop are all too often time wasting, even misleading. The prospective owner will often mount and handle these guns in a different manner to that he uses when in the field, foreshore or at a clay shooting club. It's even more difficult if the buyer has never shot a gun, and doesn't know the correct technique of gun handling. By buying locally, the buyer has always a friend at the local shop to fall back on in case of any gun or shooting problems. It is natural for the personnel in any shop to provide more willing attention to a customer who has bought his gun from them in the first place. They have a vested interest in their regular customer. Old established gun shops often have fifth or sixth generation customers from a particular family. They wish to keep these loyal people on their books and rely on the services they provide to obtain and keep their customers. It is of course perfectly possible to buy a new gun, sight unseen, from a shop in another part of the country, or visit a distant vendor to try the gun at his shooting school. But in event of any difficulty it is often easier and quicker to use local facilities. Good gun shops will be pleased to arrange a trial shoot with try-gun fitting for a customer.

The cost of alterations to improve gun fit vary dramatically. Some shops may include the cost of small alterations in the price of a gun. It is rare that a tyro buying a first gun can be provided with instant gun fit in one lesson. The fitter will first help the client to fit himself to the gun being tried, encouraging the client to develop his own most comfortable stance and style. This procedure ensures the gun will fit the shooter without him having to fit himself to the gun, resulting in a well-fitted gun which is a pleasure to own and shoot. Makers of 'best' guns are fully aware of this. When building a new gun for a client they ascertain the approximate fitting by means of skilled try-gun usage. Then as the building of the gun progresses, and while the gun is still 'in the white' the customer will be taken back to the shooting school as many times as required, until the makers and their fitter-coach are completely satisfied the gun fit is as perfect as possible.

## Buying a Gun off the Peg

Mr Average can often be fitted very well when buying new or indeed secondhand guns off the peg. With application on the part of client and fitter-coach a good fit should be achieved. Personnel at good gun shops will not provide a gun bent and butchered about to enable it to point correctly if or when the customer ill mounts it in some peculiar fashion of his or her own. The fitter will show the beginner exactly where in the shoulder pocket to mount the gun, also informing his client if the gun is being wrongly mounted. It is all too easy for a novice to mount the gun in

*A client trying an s/s gun on the Holland high tower*

**How not to mount a fitted gun**

such a manner that hitting targets is made more difficult. Many mount the butt with the muzzles still pointing towards the ground. When this happens the muzzles must then be whirled wildly to catch the target. A good fitter-coach will not condone this ineptitude. Moreover he can and will demonstrate how it should be done. Note how the muzzles are placed on the line of the high driven target with the shooter's eyes looking directly over the muzzles to assist accurate corelationship of target and gun point.

Given good after sales service, one should expect to pay market prices, not less. Gun shops have to price their guns competitively. Otherwise they will not sell. A new gun has all its working life in front of it.

## Buying Secondhand Guns from the Trade

Secondhand guns may have had little use, or they may have been sadly maltreated, ill maintained and be badly worn out-of-proof wrecks. When prepared and submitted for proof it is not unknown for such death-traps to blow up. Safer happening at the proof-house than in its owner's hands.

One can find secondhand guns with a known history which are good buys. The beginner can rely only on the integrity of the gun shop. Some sportsmen and women change their guns as a result of their own idiosyncrasies – more often than Henry the Eighth changed his wives. Such people are called 'straw clutchers' in the gun trade. Their discarded guns have often had little use, are in nearly new condition, and good value for money. There are other old guns which although once of good quality have been tarted up, with badly tightened actions. Such guns should not be bought. To sum up, most guns bought through a legitimate gun shop will be fair value. In the rare case of these guns giving trouble, the gun shop that sold the gun will rectify the problem rapidly.

## Buying Secondhand Guns Privately

Guns bought privately which malfunction create problems. The vendor may be well versed in guns, or he may not know the true condition of a gun he sells. Although it is an offence to sell an out-of-proof gun, it is better not to buy one, and then have the hassle of rectifying mistakes. The prudent buyer will insist on having any guns offered privately vetted and valued by a reputable gun shop *before* purchase. The price charged for this service is small compared with the protection provided.

## Buying by Auction

There are many reputable auctioneers with their own gauges and micrometers who know the proof laws well. Guns brought in for auction sale are carefully gauged and vetted. There will be a fair description of the gun in the catalogue. Even the choke constriction can be checked. A pre-sale viewing time is usual; the prudent purchaser will seek advice from the auctioneer regarding the condition of any lot, its reserve price and other relevant information.

The prices realized can often vary greatly, the auctioneer is there to obtain a fair price for the seller of the gun. If there are two or more willing bidders he will keep taking bids. It is up to the buyer to do his homework

*Lining up muzzles and targets during gun mounting* (Apsley S.S.)

first. Even if he does buy a gun at a reasonable price at auction the probable cost of having a fitting lesson and any subsequent stock alterations still have to be taken into consideration.

## A Trial Shoot

An hour at a shooting ground with fitter-coach, try-gun and cartridges can cost £50 to £60. There is the cost of alterations, if any. So it is best to buy where one can try. The shooter's body takes the recoil. Shooting a gun helps any customer, even a tyro, assess its compatibility. It is better to find out before purchase if gun and shooter are incompatible. Time and money expended at a shooting school is well spent and usually results in a gun which fits its owner and is eminently suitable for the type of shooting favoured.

# 4
# The Shotgun Stock and Fore-end

## STOCK AND FORE-END SHAPES

SHOTGUN stocks and fore-ends have become much more sophisticated over the years. The use of the stock bolt fixing and modern machinery to produce machine-made stocks in many shapes has encouraged a proliferation of stock and fore-end shapes.

All these shapes have their devotees for reasons good or bad, the choice of a certain shape being sometimes due to a shooter's idiosyncrasies. Many years ago one of our top DTL shots fitted a piece of sheepskin and its wool on to and over the comb of his trap-gun. He was a splendid shot and was at that time on a winning streak. Many other competitors saw this woolly comb raiser and did likewise. Those whose trap-guns had stocks with low combs probably shot better. Others found the addition did nothing to help their subsequent performance. Joe Wheater, one of our all time greats, supplied rubber comb raisers which helped those who had low-combed stocks. He, however, was an expert fitter and only fitted them to guns which needed such additions to help their owners obtain a better gun fit.

### Temporary Alterations to Comb Height and Shape

There are now numerous methods of comb lifting on a temporary basis until the best shape and height of the comb and butt plate is established. Then and only then should the experimenting owner, working in

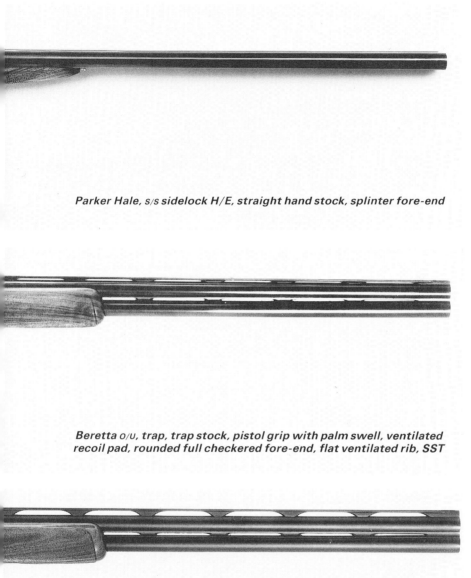

*Parker Hale, s/s sidelock H/E, straight hand stock, splinter fore-end*

*Beretta o/u, trap, trap stock, pistol grip with palm swell, ventilated recoil pad, rounded full checkered fore-end, flat ventilated rib, SST*

*Beratta o/u, trap stock with Monte Carlo comb, pistol grip, palm swell, ventilated recoil pad, rounded full checkered fore-end, raised rib, SST.*

conjunction with his fitter-coach, enlist the services of a skilled stocker to transform the temporary comb into a comb permanently fitted to its owner stock.

## Permanent Alterations to Comb Height and Shape

The original comb is removed, the stock prepared, a piece of wood carefully inletted into the stock. This and stock are then shaped to the measurements, the stock balanced and finally finished in such a manner – perhaps as a Monte Carlo type – that it is difficult to see the added comb.

All this is a far cry from the tyro who usually regards the gun stock as merely a shaped piece of wood, interposed between the shooter's shoulder pocket and the action and barrel(s) and the fore-end as the place where one positions the front hand when using the gun. As we have already seen the stocker-gun-fitter-coach knows only too well there is much more than that to this complex subject. An excellent full-length book on this is *The Shotgun Stock* by R. Arthur, which covers the subject in depth. (See Bibliography.)

## The Interchangeable Stock

These days many imported guns are offered with a choice of stock. Usually such stocks are fixed to the action by means of a stock bolt. They are completely interchangeable and can be switched in minutes, all required being a turnscrew and a socket spanner.

*Beretta semi-automatic with 3 interchangeable stocks, right hand Monte Carlo, right hand Sporter, left hand Sporter, screw-in chokes, choke tool, turnscrew, socket spanner for stock nut, stock spacers, recoil pads, trigger assembly pin remover*

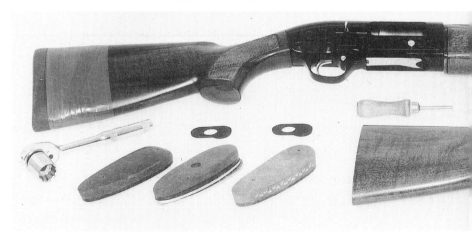

**Stock for** o/u **with inletted Monte Carlo comb** *(courtesy of J. Wills, Gunsmith and Custom Stocker)*

## Stock Butt and Recoil Pads

These also come in many shapes.

These pads can be moved up or down, also angled sideways to produce a certain amount of cast-off or -on.

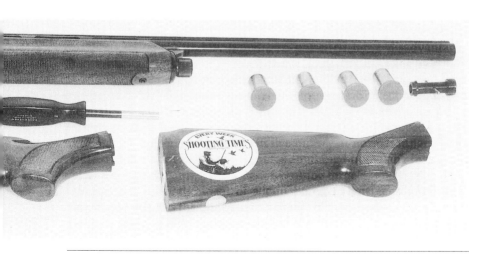

*Beretta (top) and Winchester trap stocks, recoil pads and turnscrew*

## The Advantages and Disadvantages of the Various Stock and Fore-end Shapes

The straight hand stock has long been popular with those who shoot live quarry and favour the use of two triggers. The theory behind this thinking is as follows: Guns with double triggers and straight hand stocks allow the trigger hand to be slid slightly backwards along the stock hand/grip after one has fired the front trigger, enabling one to press the rear trigger and fire the second barrel. This is not always true. Short-fingered shots may have to move their hand rearwards.

Those with longer fingers need not move their hand when firing double triggers. The technique for those with a normal-sized hand and finger length is to so position their trigger hand on the stock grip that the pad of their first finger is placed on the front trigger. Pressure applied results in firing the first barrel. With the trigger hand still static, they then use the crack of the first joint of their trigger finger to pull the rear trigger and fire their second barrel.

Stock length, the shape of the stock hand and the length of comb all need considering, as does the position of the shooter's front hand. Those with arthritic wrists may find that the angle at which the trigger hand is held with a straight hand stock is uncomfortable. Others find they have a tendency to cant guns with straight hand stocks. This canting is more pronounced with a long-toed stock and a well-nourished shooter. The beefy muscular shooter with well-developed pectoral muscles is another who tends to cant his gun if that gun has a long-toed stock. When shooting such a gun he too finds the stock toe transmits most of the gun recoil straight back into the shoulder pocket through about a one square inch of stock surface area. Another factor is the thickness and section shape of the straight hand stock.

## Grips

### The London grip
This is of a slightly oval or diamond shape and has found much favour for driven game.

### The half pistol grip
This is a compromise. Favoured by those who do not like a straight hand or the other extreme. The devotees of this shape claim more control than when shooting a straight hand stock but believe they still have a less cramped trigger-hand position than with a full pistol grip. Those with short fingers who need to move their trigger hand when shooting two triggers find hand movement easier with a half pistol grip.

### The Prince of Wales grip
This is similar to the half pistol and less restrictive than the full pistol grip, and the same criteria apply.

### The full pistol grip
This is favoured by those who prefer a single or single selective trigger. Ideally the hand of a full pistol grip stock should be shaped to exactly fit and fill the trigger hand of its owner, thus ensuring the hand is always comfortably positioned in exactly the same place. This exact position is an asset. (See Chapter 14.)

If the circumference of the grip is too large compared with the size of the trigger hand, the trigger finger may be wood bound, and pressing against the side of the stock hand with the finger stretching to reach the trigger, may cause finger pressure sideways instead of straight backwards. This sideways pressure increases the pull required for trigger release. If the stock hand is too small, the trigger hand will find it difficult to obtain a firm grip; if the pistol or half pistol grip is placed far back in relation to the trigger position in the trigger guard, the trigger finger may be placed anywhere. This sloppy placement encourages a varying trigger pressure as described above and results in inconsistent trigger pulling and timing.

## The Fore-end

There are many shapes available. The splinter fore-end is popular in this country on side by side guns. It does have a disadvantage: sportsmen who wish to fire many cartridges quickly will find the barrels get too hot to

*Lancaster four-barrelled action (courtesy of J. Wills, Gunsmith and Custom Stocker)*

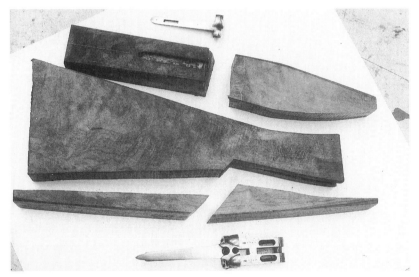

*Band sawn stock blank for Lancaster four barrel action, fore-end iron*

hold and they have to either fit a hand guard and/or wear a glove. Some prefer the beavertail fore-end which keeps the hand away from hot barrels.

## Type of Wood

This is usually walnut, obtainable in many grades from the ordinary straight grained to the exotic with its beautiful figure. 'Best' gun makers spend much time and money searching for super-quality blanks. These may cost four figures or more per blank and must add to the cost of the gun. Even so it is money well spent.

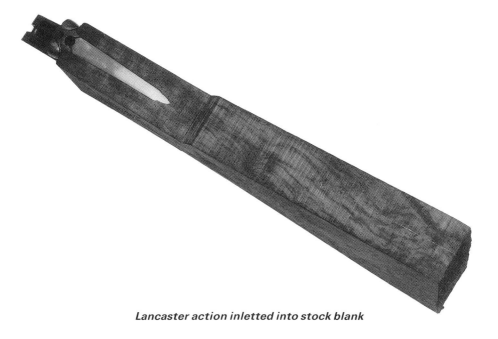

*Lancaster action inletted into stock blank*

## Stock Finish

This can range from the best London dull oil to the spray-on polyurethane type. One pays one's money. Most people, myself included, regard a 'best' London oil finish on top quality walnut as a thing of beauty and a joy for ever. When one considers that a properly maintained 'best' gun has been known to efficiently digest more than a million cartridges and also at the end of that time is worth much more than it cost originally, one can appreciate just how the use of quality woodwork enhances such guns.

*The finished article with best oil finish to stock and fore-end. The barrels are still in the white; when they are blued – a joy for ever (courtesy of J. Wills, Gunsmith and Custom Stocker)*

## The Custom Stocker

These people are artists and few and far between. But given the best grade of wood they can transform a stock blank into a thing of beauty and joy to its owner. The illustration here shows what an expert can do. The gun is a rare 4-barrelled Lancaster gun made many years ago. Due to the larger than normal size of the action the stock head had also to be larger to contain all the works. The result after many many hours of highly-skilled craftsmanship shows how the stock blank was band sawn to a rough shape, then the action, etc. fitted, the stock made off with an integral cheek piece and the gun balanced. The whole of the woodwork was 'best' oil finished. This is a superb example of the stocker's art which the fortunate owner will doubtless treasure. The barrels are still in the white.

# 5

# Choosing a Gun

## CHOICE OF BORE

THE bore or gauge of a gun is based on the inside diameter of the gun barrel(s) at 9 in from the breech and is calculated by the number of pure lead spherical balls – each of which fits the bore – that makes up one Imperial pound in weight. Therefore a 12 bore gun would have a barrel of a diameter which would accept 12 lead balls which when weighed en masse would weigh 1 lb. The 16 bore would accept 16 lead balls, the 20 bore 20 balls, and so on, the exception being the .410. Here this figure is the actual calibre and shows the barrel internal diameter in decimals of an inch.

I have met lots of sportsmen and women who began their shooting career with a single barrel .410. These guns are available with three chamber lengths. The 2 in which takes a $\frac{5}{16}$ oz. shot load, $2\frac{1}{2}$ in which takes $\frac{7}{16}$ oz. shot load, and the 3 in cased cartridge which takes up to a $\frac{5}{8}$ oz. load. Due to these shot loads being small compared to a 12 bore all too often .410 guns have barrels which are tightly choked. These can cause great problems for even an experienced shot. As for the novice, the owning and shooting of any full choked gun means the dice are firmly loaded against him. This when one is considering the taking of live quarry or sporting clays at the normal distances which are usually from 20–30 yds. The shot pattern diameter from a correctly bored full choke barrel of any gauge at 25 yds whether 12 right through to .410 will be on average 21 in. This provides an area of roughly 340 square in. The 32 in

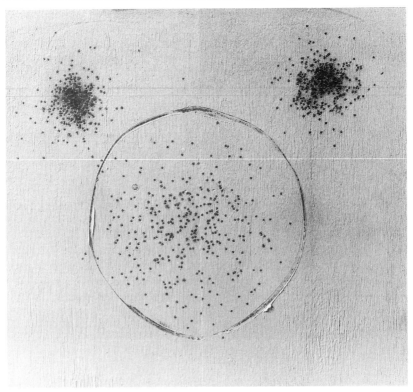

**Two patterns from full choke and one from improved cylinder borings.
All shot at a distance of 20 yds**

spread produced by an improved cylinder bored barrel at 25 yds gives a
pellet area of roughly 800 square in. A vast difference.

Moreover in the case of the 3 in × .410 cartridge the proportions of the
diameter of the shot column compared to its length can result in greater
pellet deformation, maybe even 'balling' of the shot. There are two
causes of this balling: one is by the welding together of the shot pellets
caused by a combination of high pressure and very soft shot; the other is
the fusion of the pellets by the hot gases getting past the wadding due to
poor obturation and into the shot charge. The latter can occur when a
short cased 2 in cartridge is fired from a 3 in-chambered .410, the
difference in case length and chamber depth causing poor obturation.
The evidence can be seen on lots of shooting school pattern plates by the
indentations caused by balling. Balled shot if it is placed plumb centre on
a game bird will cause almost total destruction. Moreover balled shot
travels vast distances. Burrard, in *Modern Shotgun*, writes of a case
reported in the *British Medical Journal*, 1888, of shot balling and striking a
bystander in the face and breaking his jaw at a 133-yd distance. The
same shot killed a pheasant.

It is not generally realized by the tyro that the proof pressure from .410 by 3 in cartridges is so great that such 3 in-chambered .410 guns are proofed at 5 tons per square inch. A vast difference to the standard 12 bore proofing of 3 tons for a $2\frac{1}{2}$ in-chambered 12 bore gun.

The .410 gun does have a few points in its favour for the beginner. The recoil is small and often being single-barrelled it may be an inexpensive gun to buy. For the reasons above it is a difficult gun even for an expert to shoot competently. Not for nothing do our American cousins dub these guns 'idiot sticks'.

A better gun for most young beginners is the 28 bore. Experience has shown that a well-regulated 28 bore gun with improved cylinder boring with a $2\frac{1}{2}$ in cartridge and $\frac{9}{16}$ oz. shot load will account for live quarry or clay targets up to distances of 30 yds.

For ladies or normal adult males a correctly fitted 12 bore gun should be first choice. There is a wide selection of shot loads in 12 bore cartridges. Eley make cartridges for standard 12 bore guns with $2\frac{1}{2}$ in chambers with shot loads from $\frac{7}{8}$ oz. through to $1\frac{3}{16}$ oz. The formula should be – the heaviest gun which can be comfortably handled and the lightest load. When expertise has been acquired, the amount of shot load can be increased if required.

The weight of the shot charge does not replace accuracy. Greener's advice a century ago, 'there is no substitute for placing the pellet pattern on target', still holds true.

## OTHER FACTORS

For all practical purposes it matters little to most people whether the barrels are placed side by side, or on the top of one another as with the over and under gun. Fashion has quite a bearing on this question. To generalize, the side by side will swing slightly better on crossing shots, especially if there is a strong cross wind blowing. Some who have always shot an over and under may find they do not see driven targets or live quarry if they then change to a side by side. The reason being their other eye does not see 'round the barrels' so easily. Others find the stacked barrels of the over and under do obtrude on crossing shots and encourage the other eye to take over causing cross firing.

There is still a slight resistance to the use of an over and under on a few game shoots; this is diminishing and given safe behaviour by the owner the superposed gun should be readily accepted at formal game shoots. The cost of guns of the same quality varies little between side by side and over and under. Regardless of what some pundits claim, a skilled stocker – given the correct stock dimensions by an expert fitter-coach – can produce a well-fitted gun for the owner regardless of gun type.

It is best to buy an ejector gun if possible. These eject empty fired cases as and when the gun is opened. A non-ejector simply raises both fired and unfired cases as the gun is opened. If one is buying a non-ejector, it is worthwhile checking the amount of this cartridge case lift. With some guns the unfired cartridge or fired case is only lifted $\frac{1}{16}$ in, making it difficult for cold or gloved hands to take out live or empty cases. For rough shooting or wildfowling and, also for clay target shooting, except for flushes or flurries, there is little need for ejectors.

Sooner or later as a natural progression the sportsman will be invited to a good driven game shoot. At such times the ejector gun will assist one to take more birds with less hassle.

## Boxlock or Sidelock

There are more moving parts in the average sidelock, and usually sidelocks cost more to produce. A well-designed and -constructed action of either type can be tuned to produce a sweet functioning gun with first-class trigger pulls. Gun weight, barrel length and weight of shot load should be considered in relation to the physique of the shooter. Experience has shown the average game shooter performs very well with a side by side or over and under 12 bore with a weight of between $6\frac{1}{2}$ to 7 lb, the barrel lengths most favoured being 28 in. Bored improved cylinder and half choke, fuelled with a 1 oz. load, such a combination should – if pointed right – be ample for game birds to 40 yds. Too much choke results in smashed birds when taken at the usual 20–25 yd ranges.

Although this is best left to a gunsmith the locks on a sidelock are more easily removed, all that is required being a turnscrew and the know-how to use it.

Boxlocks are not so easily dismantled although it is equally easy to remove the stock by means of a turnscrew and socket spanner on an over and under gun; this does allow one a chance to inspect most of the works. Even so Mr Average will be well advised to leave the periodic strip and cleaning of his beloved gun to an expert gunsmith. This will be money well spent and should ensure one is using a safely maintained efficient working gun.

## The Safety Catch

In reality there is no such thing. The action of the fitment named the safety catch usually only blocks the trigger blades and prevents any pressure on the trigger(s) releasing the sear(s) out of bent, which in turn allows the hammer/tumbler to fall and strike the firing pin. What the

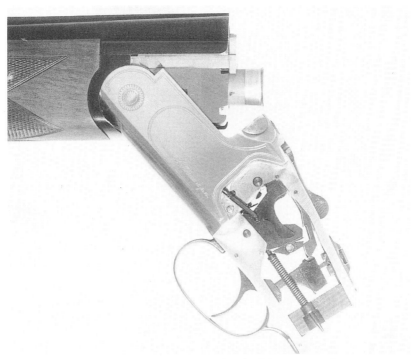

*It is easy to remove the stock on a o/u boxlock by means of a turnscrew and socket spanner to inspect the internals*

normal safety catch does not and indeed by its design cannot do, is to prevent the sear(s) jarring out of bent if the gun is dropped or bumped. Even sidelock guns with intercepting safety sears may have their sears jarred out of bent if dropped.

There are two types of safety catch. One is the manual or non automatic catch. As implied, the owner physically moves the safety slide or thumb piece to 'safe' or 'fire'. Popular on guns for clay target shooting. The other type is the automatic catch. As the gun is opened, the safety slide/thumb piece is automatically moved to the 'on safe' position. It stays put in that position until moved by the owner.

When the gun has been loaded and closed, the onus is on the owner to slide the thumb piece into the 'fire' position. Those who wish to understand the workings of safety catches should consult their regular gunsmith. They will find him ready to demonstrate on a partially stripped down action. A 'safety catch' does not make a loaded gun safe. No thinking sportsman relies on his safety catch.

## Triggers

These can be double, single, or single selective. Contrary to popular belief a single trigger is not faster in use, but it does facilitate shooting in gloves. Double triggers give one the instant choice of any difference in barrel choking. Single triggers do not. Short-fingered shooters and others who experience a bruised second finger will usually find switching to a single trigger will cure this problem.

## Chokes and choke tubes

The introduction of interchangeable screw-in choke tubes must be one of the success stories of recent years. These allow the knowledgeable sportsman to choose the best combination of choke tube and cartridge load to suit his quarry or clay target.

## New or Secondhand?

It is difficult sometimes to choose between buying new or secondhand. Most guns, whether new or not are keenly priced. Some gun shops provide a fitting and do small alterations in the price of the gun. Before purchase it is prudent to test fire the gun of one's choice. In fact the correct place to sort out any shooting problem is at a good school in the presence of an expert gun fitter-coach. They will have met similar problems many times before and can describe the fault and prescribe the remedy. Cradock's law is, 'the owner must have suitable equipment, and proven confidence obtained through shooting school experience in his ability to use it. Unless this is so, a competent performance, with pleasure of ownership and the shooting of the gun will be unlikely.'

# 6
# The First Gun

## THE YOUNG BEGINNER

ONE is often asked, 'What is the best age at which to start shooting a shotgun?'. There can be no hard and fast rule. Humans are complex beings. As for the young entry, some are precocious, well developed physically and mentally and are ready to try anything. Others are under developed, diffident, and as a result of previous amateurish attempts, maybe all too often scared or at the least apprehensive at the mere thought of shooting a gun. Those with shooting parents, who have previously accompanied father while he has been shooting are usually at an advantage. As the young are eager to emulate their elders, it is necessary therefore for all of us to be on best behaviour at all times. Youngsters soon assimilate much knowledge. Whether the example set is good or bad rests with the parent.

For all beginners, the motto must be to make haste slowly. Unless and until the young person is interested and really wants to take up shooting, it is wrong to throw him in at the deep end regardless. The old country method of teaching farm boys the ropes had little to recommend it, the technique favoured being to shout a few sketchy instructions as loudly as possible. This confused the youth who, having been held up to ridicule so often in the past, dared not ask for detailed explanations of said instructions. Due to this stupidity the task was tackled with a bad grace and ill done. All of which gave the bullying overseer another chance to explain to all within earshot just how stupid was the youth and how useless his efforts.

The physical strength of the young entry plus the characteristics of the gun to be used must be considered. If he or she is keen all is well, but if the exercise is carried out begrudgingly to please father or uncle, it is better for all to postpone the acquisition and shooting of a gun until real desire develops. As advised in the previous chapter a 28 bore gun is usually a good choice for the beginner. I have known keen 10-year-old youngsters who handled 28 bore guns well, and loved every minute of their lessons.

In some sporting families there is often a small bore heirloom of a gun which has been used by the young entry for the past half century. Some of these guns are family treasures and have been carefully maintained by the local gun shop. These guns will be in safe condition. Other guns will have been lent out in the distant past to another branch of the family. These guns may often have been misused, left uncleaned and badly stored. Even a 'best' gun will suffer from such barbarism. Unknown guns should be treated with suspicion and always vetted before use by a local gunsmith.

Non-shooting parents or guardians should seek advice at the same time on which cartridges should be used in any gun. This advice should be in writing, and kept in the gun case. All too often, little Johnny has perused cartridge adverts and decided the heavier loads must be best; he will try and persuade some doting aunt or uncle to buy cartridges which are quite unsuitable, often even dangerous to use for the gun in question.

Special consideration must be given to .410 single barrel guns. Before the war many low-priced folding single barrel .410 guns were imported.

***Boy with his first .410 gun. Note the wide leaning backward stance, second finger used to pull the trigger***

*A few years later, the same boy with 28 bore gun. Note the improved close stance and style. First finger along guard ready to move and press trigger. Barrels with muzzles held ready to collect the high bird as it appears*

Some were reasonably well made, others not so. Some had 2 in chambers, and may have suffered years of neglect. To load one of these old wrecks with $2\frac{1}{2}$ in or 3 in cartridges and fire it is foolhardy. So seek advice first.

Those very young who are really keen, but physically not up to handling a 28 bore, can be entered to clay shooting by means of a single .410 which has been checked and is in safe shooting condition. These guns when in the hands of a novice are not good tools with which to shoot live quarry but they can be used to inculcate gun safety in the young and to effect on sporting clays. Better a chipped target than a pricked live quarry. For those who have no family gun to borrow, the local gun shop is the sensible place at which to seek advice. First visit the shop without the youngster, discuss with the expert exactly what amount of money is available, and what should be expected from the young person. The advice obtained will provide most of the answers. Then make an appointment to take in 'Young Sir' or 'Madam' to the shop. Do allow plenty of time. To dash in the shop, with the car left outside on double yellow lines, is self defeating and unfair to the gun shop, resulting in time wasted and money ill spent. Having inspected what guns are available, their cost, and suitability as far as price and purpose are concerned, the next step is to arrange a visit to the local shooting school where selected guns can be trial fired. Most shooting coaches enjoy schooling the young entry and will soon have their client at ease and enjoying the visit. Sometimes the cost of this first visit may be included in the price of any gun which is subsequently purchased. But if there is no sale it is of course normal for a charge to be made for use of ground, targets, cartridges, etc.

Most coaches prefer to use first a snap cap or dummy cartridge in the chamber of whatever gun is being tried. The gun will be pre-mounted in the shoulder pocket by the coach. It is vital to provide the beginner with trigger-pressing practice on snap caps before a live round is chambered. The reason is elementary. When one drives a strange car, the brakes are gently tried to check the amount of pressure required to apply the brakes smoothly. Clients who have never fired a gun may apply far too much pressure on the trigger. If they do this with a loaded gun, that gun will be fired prematurely. The gun may not be fully mounted. The result of all this may be that the youngster is startled by the noise and hurt by the recoil. He or she is also scared and most of us would feel the same in like circumstances.

## FITTING THE FIRST GUN

The visit to the school allows the fitter-coach to size up the young entry. He will be checked for master eye; if he is right-handed and has a right master eye, all will be well. If his master eye is on the opposite side, one must decide whether the wrong eye has to be closed, or whether it is easier for the gun to be shot off the same shoulder as the master eye. For most beginners who are keen this switching of shoulders comes easy; even in later life there have been many instances where the shooter has switched shoulders to match his master eye, usually with beneficial result.

If there are other sons or daughters in the family to follow the first young entry and a gun has to be specially purchased and, as so often is the case, this gun has a stock which is too long, it makes sense to ask the stocker to keep the piece of wood which he removes from the stock. Then when the youngster grows that piece of removed stock can be refitted, usually by means of a couple of wood screws, to be removed once more in the future as and when the next youngster comes along.

It will be stressed in this book, shooting is a sport of responsibility. Anyone taking up the sport must cultivate this attitude to their guns. Safer gun handling must be cultivated at all times until muzzle awareness comes as natural as breathing and ensures no closed gun is ever pointed in an unsafe direction. This is regardless of whether it is loaded or not. It is a joy to teach safe gun handling to the young. If correctly entered these youngsters will have no bad habits to unlearn. Thus making it all the easier to acquire and cultivate the do's of safe gun handling.

# 7
# Guns and Cartridges for Game,

## THE LATE BEGINNER

THIS is a vast subject, countless books and millions of words having been written on the pros and cons. Fortunates like myself and countless others who have been privileged to live and grow up in our lovely countryside rarely understand or are fully aware of the many problems which arise when a city dweller decides late in life to take up live shooting. The countryman or woman who has been brought up amongst a shooting family is doubly blessed. Learning to shoot safely, observing the shooting code, is and always has been an ongoing process. In the days of one's youth any time spent amongst shooting people was precious and eventually resulted in one automatically conforming with the mostly unwritten etiquette of good manners and safe gun handling, respect for the quarry and the countryside.

This present chapter is not for these lucky people. It is addressed to the many who, through no fault of their own, take up live shooting later in life, usually after making a success of their business or profession. The wiser realize they have a lot to learn. Their experience of life has taught them that all etiquette is based on good manners and common sense. So, they first take a series of shooting lessons, thus ensuring they will be taught how to conform, i.e. behave safely and shoot competently. Not until their coach passes them fit to partake in live shooting will they accept any game shooting invitations. When passed competent performers they still make haste slowly and first arrange to attend a couple of shoots as an observer in the company of an experienced game shot. They will watch how he conforms, how he carries his unloaded gun in its sleeve cover between drives, keeps quiet at all times ('Game can Hear and Game can See'), and how all his shooting is directed towards safe ground devoid of other life. After this initial grounding and to make doubly certain they will take a coach along to their first couple of shoots to ensure their behaviour and gun handling is safely correct. All of this is but prudent common sense. It is difficult enough for the experienced to take note of the foregoing. In addition, there is always the thorny question of which bird to take. All too often birds will be coming very quickly. When first seen at maybe 70 yds their line of flight and angle of approach seem to indicate they will fly straight overhead. Yet a slight side wind, a shooter who shoots hatless and with a bald shining pate which can act as an unwanted flanker, and many other factors all have a bearing.

Those really high birds coming off the top of a high down or escarpment and gliding slightly downhill on set wings nearly all have a slight curl. They are also travelling much faster than one realizes. Always if there is any doubt as to whether a bird is too low and out of range, it is far better left unshot. For birds which are drifting to the next gun, it makes sense to call 'your bird' to that adjoining gun. For those first few days the coach can be a tower of strength and the tyro will learn much. He may also be saved a lot of embarrassment.

It is regrettable there still exists the myth of the 'natural shot'. It cannot be stressed too often there is no such animal. Most humans, who have good visual acuity, and are well coordinated physically, will with good coaching from day one, rapidly become safe competent shots. I believe that this has always been so. One of the finest shots we have ever acknowledged was inconsistent and incompetent until he was taught to align, and be aware of target-barrel relationship. My own experience and that of countless other coaches bears this out. Most coaches also agree that the myth of the natural shot dies slowly. It has always been surprising that hard-headed business men, who insist on their chauffeur being correctly trained to drive the big company car, and not allowing a beginner to drive them, will cheerfully spend much money buying a gun. Then, without one lesson in gun handling, they blithely go off game shooting, where all too often they are a menace and a misery to themselves and other unfortunates within 300 yds. Given time and money, anyone as described above, with normal eyesight, coordination, and application, can be taught to shoot competently and safely. Shooting is not a natural sport like running but it can be taught. Regardless of age, the complete novice with no faults to correct can be more easily taught to shoot than some self-taught person who has developed many faults: faults which he has to shed, all of which takes time. To buy the best one can afford, have it fitted, and then be taught to shoot safely and well makes for good economic sense.

## GUN WEIGHT, BARREL LENGTH AND CARTRIDGE

A gun handled in a shop may feel ideal: fast handling, easy swinging and wholly desirable. To take that same gun to a school and shoot even 25 cartridges can produce a different and uncomfortable response. Gun weight should suit the physical build of the owner. Heavier guns with longer barrels are often more stable performers. Only by trial while shooting targets can one establish a satisfactory equation of gun/ carriage/shot load. The driven game shooter may fire many cartridges during a day and in the season. If he is under gunned as to gun weight, and shoots heavy load cartridges, his shoulder will suffer. Worse, his performance and enjoyment will be diminished. The average game gun weighs 6–7 lb. Barrels can be from 25–30 in.

Barrel boring for game or rough shooting, walked up or driven: improved cylinder in one barrel and not more than half choke in the other is ample for quarry taken at ordinary ranges of up to 40 yds. Shot size: 3–5 pellets of 6, $6\frac{1}{2}$ or 7 placed on the front end of the quarry should cleanly bring a game bird to the bag at up to 40 yds distance. The popular game cartridge similar to Impax with its 1 oz. load will outperform the average shot at normal game shooting ranges. The shooting school will provide sufficient answers to enable the shooter decide what is best.

### The Rough Shooter

The rough shooter may walk many miles in one day and fire few cartridges. Due to this amount of walking, gun weight can be a problem, although recoil should not as few cartridges are fired. Again a compromise has to be found. The majority of rough shooters often take their quarry at slightly greater distances than does the driven game shot. Such will favour slightly heavier loads, having established that the few cartridges fired allow the shooting of such loads without too much discomfort. The elderly rough shooter or wildfowler will often select as light a gun as possible because of the miles he has to carry it. Each has to work out his own best combination of cartridge and weapon. As I have written before, it is the shooter's shoulder that passes judgement. This will relay the information regarding the amount of gun recoil being transmitted into his shoulder to that individual.

One of the most successful cartridges for rough shooting or wildfowling ever produced was the Eley Maximum. This was designed to be fired through a game gun with $2\frac{1}{2}$ in chambers and which had been proved for $1\frac{1}{8}$ oz. shot load. Originally the shot load was $1\frac{1}{4}$ oz. and in the days of my youth I shot many many of these heavier loaded 12 bore $1\frac{1}{4}$ oz. cartridges. These were a fine cartridge. The modern Maximum with its $1\frac{3}{16}$ oz. load seems to be equally effective.

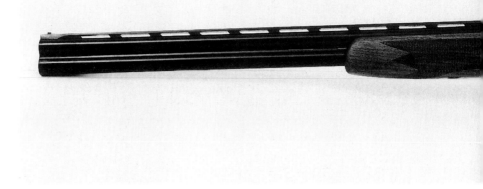

Most rough shooters will find the ideal gun weight lies between $6\frac{1}{2}$–7 lb. with the cartridge loaded to suit one's specific requirements. Barrel lengths and boring are similar to those of the game shooter. The standard 28 in length barrels are very popular, and they always sell easily when the time comes for disposal.

## The Wildfowler

The wildfowler should choose his gun after due consideration of his own capabilities in field craft. Those with good field craft shooting in favourable conditions which allow them to get much closer to their wildfowl may find their favourite game or rough shooting weapon does provide adequate performance.

There are surprisingly many wildfowlers who favour the big bore guns. Unfortunately there are but few who can take advantage of this extra firepower by placing their patterns on the front end of long distance birds. The 8 bore cartridge is no longer made by Eley. But it is still possible to buy specialist custom cases for 8 and even 4 bore guns at a price.

The 8 bore shot load is around 2 oz., the 4 bore load around 4 oz. There are few who can place an 8 bore pattern on birds at 60 yds, even fewer can shoot a 4 bore accurately enough to use its killing pattern at 80 yds. I knew a gentleman way back in the 1930s who was in his 70s then, and being a man of means spent many hours wildfowling. Game shooting interested him not at all. It was geese he was after. Decoy he would not. His self-imposed bag limit was two birds per day. When he had reached his limit he would just watch the geese come in. Due to a lifetime's experience he could cleanly kill his birds out to 80 yds with his single 4 bore. But only if the weather was calm. To stand behind the old man was an experience: supposing that the goose was a long crosser, the old man's barrels could be seen swinging on the anticipated flight line

*o/u **game gun** (Lanber)*

*s/s **game guns** (Parker-Hale)*

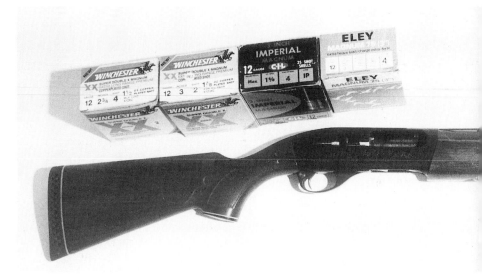

*Remington semi-automatic 3 in magnum and 3 in cartridges*

until they seemed to be almost pointing in the next parish. There would be a boom, a sheet of flame, a cloud of smoke and, after what seemed about 2 seconds, that bird would crumple and fall.

This sportsman was the exception, I believe; for most wildfowlers who wish to take their quarry at up to 60 yds ranges the best bet is the 3 in × 12 bore gun proofed to take 3 in magnum cartridges. These are loaded with $1\frac{7}{8}$ oz. of buffered shot. There are 12 bore 3 in-chambered magnum semi-automatics such as the Beretta which can digest heavy loads. There are also 12 bore double o/u or side by side guns which are chambered for 3 in magnum cartridges. There are magnums and magnums, and any reader must seek advice on cartridges and shot loads from his gun shop. The expert in the shop will examine the gun and advise what cartridge to use. It is then up to the owner to practise on long distance clay targets at up to 60 yds while shooting one of the above guns. If clay targets cannot be hit at such distances, which is very difficult indeed, it is better to brush up field craft and take one's quarry at closer ranges with a lighter gun and load. There are however and always will be many optimists regarding long range loads and long range shooting. A genuine 60 yds is a long long way. The Nilo experiments predicted 69 per cent performance with $1\frac{7}{8}$ oz. at this distance. These optimists should study these experiments as detailed in Brister's book *Shotgunning*. (See Bibliography.) Briefly, it was found that when using the most common American shot size 4 for duck shooting the effect of wind was considerable. At 60 yds with a 14.5 mph cross wind the pattern was drifted nearly 2 ft. When really high winds were blowing it was found impossible to centre the shot patterns

58

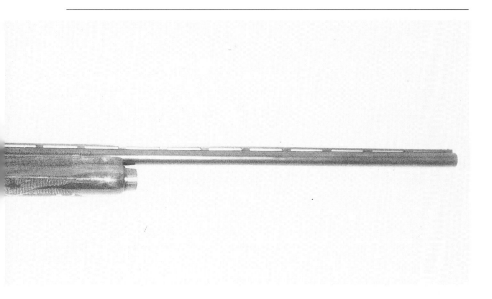

*The 4 bore gun*

accurately at 60 yds even on static targets. When the drop of the shot and the lower velocity at such distances is also considered it is understandable why so few can use these big guns and magnum loads effectively. American size 4 shot roughly equates to English size 3 which is also popular for duck and geese in this country. Barrel length for the 3 in magnum guns: usually 30 in are favoured.

## CONCLUSIONS

Good guns are available as new or secondhand for all purposes. They can be of side by side or o/u design. The actions can be boxlock or sidelock design, with or without selective ejectors, single, single selective, or double triggers. All the options are freely available.

Due to commercial pressures guns in most shops are keenly priced. When sold from a reputable gun shop they should be in good condition and value for money. It is up to the would-be purchaser to select a suitable gun after full discussion with the expert and test firing in the company of the coach. The combination of a fitted gun and compatible cartridges should help the owner to hit as much or more than he misses. But only if he plays his part and takes time out to learn to use his gun correctly. The blame for poor performance cannot be attributed to a good gun or cartridge.

The fault for any misses at normal ranges will be due to the person who is standing behind and firing the gun. It is his finger on the trigger and his decision when to pull that trigger. Any missed targets must be due to the shooter and no-one else.

# 8
# Guns and Cartridges for Clay Shooting

THESE days there are many forms of clay target shooting. Each form is termed a discipline. In the beginning 'Trap Shooting' or 'Down the Line' was the only discipline. Clay pigeon shooting was invented/designed in the late nineteenth century, the object being to provide an alternative to the pastime of live pigeon shooting in which live birds were placed in collapsible boxes or 'traps', released on a command from the shooter and fired at as they flew away. The sport of clay target/pigeon shooting has grown greatly since then. More than a million clay targets are shot at each week in this country. These disciplines can be classified in three main groups:

*Group 1*  The going-away disciplines: these are Down the Line, Automatic Ball Trap, Universal Trench and Olympic Trench.

*Group 2*  The Skeet type disciplines: these are English Skeet, ISU Skeet and American Skeet.

*Group 3*  These are English Sporting and FITASC Sporting.

Modern clay targets come in many shapes and sizes. The standard target is still normal usage for the going-away and the various skeet-type disciplines. For the sporting disciplines a mix of any available targets can be thrown. These are the standard targets: the rabbit target, which is designed to roll or bounce along the ground; the midi – a 90 mm diameter target, and mini – a much smaller target, described by some competitors as a simulated and demented aspirin; the battue – this is basically a thin disc, aerodynamically unstable which will curl, dip, slip and slide in unpredictable directions depending on prevailing wind conditions. These modern targets may be thrown on varying trajectories and distances.

All these target factors have encouraged the development of purpose-designed guns to match the needs of each group of disciplines. During the twentieth century championships in all the disciplines have been won with the help of almost every type of shotgun. In these modern days it is usually the specialist competitor who is successful. Most of these present champions understandably favour the above purpose-designed guns produced specially to suit their requirements when shooting targets in a specific discipline in one of the above groups. Due to factors of weight, a single sighting plane, choice of easily interchangeable stocks and fore-ends, screw-in chokes, cost and availability, the o/u gun is the popular choice.

## THE GUN FOR GROUP 1 DISCIPLINES

The targets thrown are all 'going away' and rising to a greater or lesser degree. They are mostly taken on the rise. Two cartridges can be fired per single target. Shooters are in squads of five or six. In the space of a few minutes a full squad will have shot at either 125 or 150 targets between them.

So the choice of the experts is an o/u gun of full weight, between 7 and 9 lb. Precision in pointing and pattern placement is essential, so the long barrel is favoured, the norm these days being 30 in or even 32 in. The top rib will be ventilated and have an anti-glare surface. These ribs come in many widths and heights. Recoil pads shaped to fit the shoulder pocket contours accurately are popular and reduce felt recoil and butt movement.

### Stock Length

Due to the gun being pre-mounted most trap-gun stocks are slightly longer than normal.

### Comb Height

Other things being equal, a quick check for comb height is to place a £1 coin flat on the top rib close to the breech. When the gun is mounted the shooter should still be just able to see the front sight apparently sitting on or over the top of the coin. Trap guns often have a small intermediate sight midway down the top rib. The fitting of this small sight provides trap shooters with an ideal sight picture, i.e., they see the front sight apparently sat on the top of the intermediate sight in a figure-of-eight

*Modern Beretta trap gun with high rib, comb, for high pattern placement*

position. Such a sight picture usually requires a high or trap-type comb and results in the pellet pattern being thrown slightly high.

Much depends on one's individual style, but guns which allow the owner to seemingly sit the target on the front sight as and when the trigger is pulled make good sense and are popular. These guns are easy to shoot, the target always being in view over the muzzle. If it is missed with the first shot, the shooter knows and can quickly fire his second barrel. He also obtains a longer perspective when looking slightly down and over his barrel, this better perspective providing a more accurate gun point.

A flat shooting gun requires the target to be 'blotted out' by the muzzles at the moment of firing. Subsequently, if that target is missed the shooter has to wait until it rises unscathed into view over the top rib. This is time consuming, resulting in late snatchy second shots being fired at more distant targets. As with all going-away targets, any errors in gun point are magnified as the target travels away from the gun. Moreover, as the targets travel further away, they lose both target speed and spin, all of which produces erratic trajectories and make them harder to hit and break.

*Modern Beretta sporting gun, flat rib and lower stock comb. Designed to shoot to point of aim*

*Shoot at actual targets to check sight picture and pattern placement*

## Chokes and Cartridges for the Going-Away Disciplines

Modern cartridges have a vastly improved performance compared with those of 50 years ago. In those days Major Burrard claimed, and mathematically proved the claim, that it required $1\frac{1}{4}$ oz. of size 7 shot and a full choke gun to be sure of breaking 100 DTL targets in a straight run. This was when shooting gun up and standing on the normal 16 yds distance firing points. At the present time we have trap shooters who are breaking 100 straights, all first barrel kills, from 27 yd firing points. This they are achieving while shooting 1 oz. loads.

All top shots carefully observe exactly how and where each target is being broken. For instance if the shot charge is only taking the underskirt or the bottom off a target, the expert will slightly alter his sight picture until he observes the shot string is either centring or grinding the top off these rising targets.

To assist this reading of pattern placement these experts often favour slightly more choke than required. The great advantage of the modern gun with its interchangeable screw-in chokes is that it allows the experienced shot to experiment with any constriction from cylinder to full choke. If he believes the targets are slightly harder than the norm, or they are flying greater distances he can fit slightly tighter choke tubes to compensate.

## Chokes for DTL targets

There are many factors which influence choice. The speed of the shooter, his visual acuity, his 'hold' in relation to the trap house roof. Two-eyed shooters can 'hold high', if they also have quick acuity and reflexes they may take their targets 5–10 yds quicker than a one-eyed person who holds low central on the back of the trap house. All must experiment and find which choking suits them best. Most shooters will find half-choke first barrel and three-quarter choke second barrel ample. Do shoot at targets, not at the pattern plate. The manner in which the targets are broken should produce very obvious answers to the experienced fitter-coach. The pattern plate is fine for establishing pattern spread, but cannot indicate shot string, whereas shooting targets does just this for the careful observer. The same criteria apply regarding choice of chokes for the other going-away disciplines. Cartridges: here the same applies. English shot sizes 6 through to 9 are legitimate. The performance of most modern cartridges is superb, but some do produce more observed recoil which in turn may increase barrel or muzzle flip. Only by trial and error while shooting targets can one decide the most suitable combination of cartridge and choke for the individual. It is essential to 'get it right' before the competition. To attend a competition with a 'this way that way mind' is a sure recipe for failure. Once the best combination of gun has been established keep it that way. Successful clay target shooting requires full concentration and no distractions.

## THE GUN FOR GROUP 2 DISCIPLINES

Skeet targets are taken inside a range of 40 yds. Usually within 20 yds, the equivalent of English shot size 9 is mandatory. The o/u is most popular, although the semi-automatic is often preferred by ladies and others susceptible to recoil.

### Gun Weight and Balance

A weight between $7-8\frac{1}{2}$ lb. is normal. As for balance, the targets are close and quick, and there is a tendency by many to check their swing when taking the first shot in order to get more quickly on to the second target. Some have found a muzzle-heavy gun is an asset, so much so that one sees guns which have had lead tape placed around their barrels and near the muzzles by their owners in an attempt to produce a muzzle-heavy gun.

### Barrels

A length of $27-28$ in is most favoured.

### Chokings

As open as possible. It is, as usual, a matter of carefully marrying the cartridge to match the barrel boring. Sometimes the cylinder bored barrel is more choosy as far as cartridges are concerned. But combined with the appropriate cartridge it will produce patterns capable of breaking any skeet target taken within legal ranges.

### Retro Chokes

These chokes are reminiscent of the pre-war Cutts compensator with its screw-on choke tubes. The retro choke has been evolved to produce a longer shot string. The experiments of Brister and many others prove that, given the correct cartridge, the shot string is lengthened by these retros. The longer shot string must be an advantage on those narrow-angle skeet targets. My own and the experiments of others indicate that felt or fibre type wads are more suitable for use in these retro-choked barrels.

## Muzzle Brakes

Modern muzzle brakes resemble the pre-war Cutts compensator, and the post-war Brno skeet gun with muzzle brake barrels. These reduce the recoil and if angled correctly can reduce muzzle flip.

## Stocks

The gun down position is mandatory for isu skeet so a well-fitted easy-to-mount gun is a must. Most favour a flat shooting gun although there are a few who successfully shoot guns which throw patterns slightly high.

## Cartridges

English 9s or their continental equivalent are mandatory. It is worthwhile by careful shooting experiments establishing the perfect marry of gun and cartridge to suit the owner.

## THE GUN FOR GROUP 3 DISCIPLINES

Sporting Targets are thrown on almost any trajectory and a wide range of target speed. The distances at which the targets are shot can vary greatly. Years ago, the usual gun choice for Sporting was a skeet gun for the close targets with a DTL type of gun being used for those going away. For FITASC Sporting the gun position is 'down', so, as usual, a well-fitted gun which can be easily mounted consistently is a must. As for the most suitable gun type there is little unanimity amongst the champions. One man won the world championship using a Remington semi-automatic; the barrel was 28 in and bored modified or half choke. Another won with a Winchester o/u with 30 in barrels with screw-in tubes bored quarter, quarter choke. That, together with the Winchester 8 shot – English equivalent size $7\frac{1}{2}$ – cartridges, has proved for one champion a winning combination. The European veteran class has been won with a Browning o/u with 30 in barrels bored cylinder and improved cylinder. The European Championship has been won with a Browning o/u with $27\frac{1}{2}$ in barrels bored skeet and skeet choke. However one must start somewhere. It is suggested the beginner tries a gun with 28–30 in barrels, o/u, weight 7–9 lb., with interchangeable screw-in chokes.

## Bend or Drop

Most eventually come to prefer a gun which has a slightly high point of pattern impact similar to that which has for decades been the standard for the British game gun. Most targets are taken on the rise so a gun stocked to produce a slight inbuilt lead helps.

## The Ideal Gun Cartridge Combination for any Group

The first essential is a well-fitted gun, with a weight which its owner can handle, and balance to suit. The cartridges will be of proven performance to suit the gun's chokings and weight and which when fired in quantity do not punish the shooter. This final combination of gun, cartridge and owner will have been fully proved to be the best possible. This being so the owner should have full confidence in both himself and his equipment. The correct matching of modern gun and cartridge to suit the requirements of shooting any discipline will always produce a more even performance than that of the best shot in the world. It logically follows that any erratic or substandard performance from a previous known reliable combination must be due entirely to the person standing behind the gun and pulling the trigger.

# 9
# *Modern Cartridges*

ONE cannot fully cover this subject in the space available, even in the period before the First World War. Griffiths, at that time manager of a large British cartridge manufacturer, estimated that to test ballistically the complete range of cartridges his firm were then producing could not be done in one person's lifetime.

Half a century ago Major G. Burrard wrote his opus *The Modern Shotgun*. This was in three volumes. Volume two was on *The Shotgun Cartridge*! In those days there were fewer brands of cartridge being made and most available in this country were home produced. Today one can buy cartridges from many countries designed for any specific purpose. Due to intense competition current prices of cartridges are lower than in the past 60 years. In the 1920s a farm worker's weekly wage was 30 shillings. For 30/– the sportsman could buy 250 12 bore cartridges. Now – 1989 – the equivalent of a modern farm worker's weekly pay packet of £100 buys 1250 cartridges.

## THE PIE-CRIMPED CARTRIDGE

A lifetime's experience leads me to believe modern cartridges produce a superb, consistent, reliable performance. More consistent than any shooter. The pie-crimped cartridge of today has no overshot card wad. This design feature has resulted in the old blown, cartwheel or doughnut type shot pattern being a thing of the past. In America, the home of trap shooting, before the advent of the pie-crimped closed cartridge there had been only three 100 straights shot from 25 yards. After the introduction of the crimp-closed cartridge and the elimination of the overshot wad, one competitor shot a 100 straight from 25 yds twice in one week. Nowadays 100 DTL straights are being shot from 25 yds with 1 oz. shot loads. This is a vast improvement compared with the 1920s when Burrard could postulate and even prove mathematically that a shooter required a $1\frac{1}{4}$ oz. load of size 7 shot pellets fired through a full-choke gun to be certain of shooting 100 straight from the 16 yds firing points.

In the old days Olympic trench clay targets were shot at using a $1\frac{1}{4}$ oz. shot load. Modern trench targets are harder and faster, yet scores are at least as high, being achieved with the modern higher performance cartridge and its lighter $1\frac{1}{8}$ oz. load. Twenty five straights are now being attained while shooting a 1 oz. load. Modern lighter loads are easier on the shooter's shoulder and kinder to the gun.

Most modern cartridge cases are plastic, being little affected by wet or damp conditions – an improvement on the old paper cases which tended to swell in damp conditions making loading and ejection difficult, often impossible. The old type roll-over crimp closures even in slightly damp conditions tended to lose their firmness resulting in lower pressures and slower pellet velocity. To fire a succession of the old type roll-over crimped cartridges from the first barrel could result in the cumulative recoil from the fired cartridges; cause the roll crimp turnover of the unfired cartridge in the second barrel to lift and become weaker in its resistance to the pressures induced when that cartridge was eventually fired, thus producing lower pressures and varying patterns. For this reason most of the old-time game and trap shooters transferred cartridges from their second barrel to the first barrel whenever they had the opportunity.

## Percussion Caps

Years ago these were made of copper. Now they are of steel, yet we experience very few misfires in spite of the millions of cartridges fired annually.

## Wadding

Years ago best cartridges used wool or felt wadding. These wads if of good quality obturate evenly and produced good results. Years of experiment have produced the modern plastic wad with its shot cup. This cup protects the pellets on the outside of the shot column from abrasion as they are propelled up the barrel, reducing malformation of pellets and the number of 'flyers' on the pattern plate. When taking close skeet targets at the usual distances such malformation matters little. In fact there is at least one school of thought which advises the use of very soft lead pellets and a type of barrel boring design which does in effect make many pellets lose their spherical shape. Other cartridges have a special wad with a centre plastic pillar. When cartridges so loaded are fired from a tightly choked barrel the resulting pattern will be much wider than is produced from normally wadded cartridges which are fired from a choke barrel. In certain conditions this can be an advantage.

Other wads may consist of a combination of fibre and plastic. The majority of modern wads have been specifically purpose-designed. The modern shooter is spoilt for choice, being able to select ammunition which will produce a wider or tighter spread than normal. This facility, in conjunction with a modern barrel with interchangeable choke tubes provides competitors with almost every conceivable option of pattern spread and performance. Warning: for certain competitions the use of spreader cartridges is not allowed. The reader should check the rules for the clay discipline which he or she is shooting.

## TESTING CARTRIDGES

To test cartridges safely requires a knowledge of explosives, accurate equipment plus meticulous use of the same. A layman must obtain professional advice from a gunsmith before he begins cartridge testing. I do not believe it possible to explain in full detail the precautions required by means of the written word. There will be those who wish to test their own cartridges regardless. My own belief is that either one of the proof houses will do a professional job at a reasonable price.

Any cartridges being tested should have been correctly stored from the time they left the factory. They must not have been exposed to extremes of heat or cold. To test cartridges which have been previously exposed to such extremes is unfair to the makers and may produce erratic unreliable results, results which may even be dangerous due to the higher pressures produced when cartridges have been stored in hot conditions. The home tester can test fire his chosen cartridges at a pattern plate at carefully measured distances. But unless he knows exactly the number of pellets in the various brands of test cartridges he cannot know whether he is testing like with like. There are some cartridges which are marked 7 shot. They may in fact be size $6\frac{1}{2}$ or even $7\frac{1}{2}$ shot. Therefore he must first have an expert open some of the test cartridges and find out what the shot size and count actually is.

The old timers knew this as well. So much so that Greener designed a shot-counting trowel to make sure that each and every cartridge had the same number of pellets in its shot charge.

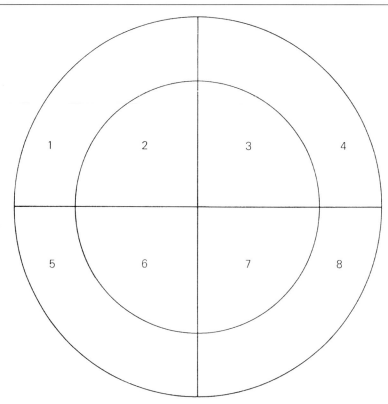

**Comparative evaluation of pattern quality by dividing the area into 8 equal segments and counting the pellets in each segment**

## The Test Gun

It is customary to fire first one cartridge through a clean barrel to foul the bore. Then each cartridge afterwards can be fired at a clean pattern plate from a measured distance and the results photographed. Photo enlargements can be produced and these photos spotted at home in peace and quiet in an evening. Then each pattern is evaluated and cartridge performance estimated.

A method used by many is to establish the centre of the pattern, then draw a 30 in diameter circle around this centre point. This centralizes the pattern within the circle. Inside this circle, and concentric within it, is scribed a circle of 21 in diameter. By means of two straight lines crossing in the circle centre the whole area contained inside the 30 in circle has been divided into eight segments of equal area. It is a simple matter to count the pellet distribution accurately. The usual distance at which one takes one's targets or quarry is decided.

*Using the 30 in diameter ring to establish pattern centre and spread*

All cartridges on test will be shot at the pattern plate at that distance using the same pair of barrels and chokings for each box of cartridges. As soon as a good combination of cartridge, shot size, and choke has been established the gun owner should eschew all others, regardless of what others may advise. This testing must be done before any live or target shooting is done for real. Greener rightly advised a century ago that a competition was not the place for experiments.

The greatest variation in performance is due to the man behind the gun. Another factor is recoil. Felt recoil is more apparent when shooting at a pattern plate and can be misleading. Therefore when a seemingly suitable cartridge/gun combination has been selected, it is worthwhile spending a couple of hours in the company of an experienced coach at a shooting school.

One can fire about the same number of cartridges on targets as would be shot either in competition or in an average day's live shooting. This may result in 100 plus being fired in quick time. The shooter's body, face and shoulder will pass on the message as to whether the recoil produced is acceptable. It is very easy to select a cartridge then subsequently find the cumulative recoil produced is too great. This results in uncomfortable and erratic shooting. Most tyros tend to use too heavy a load and too light a gun. It is better to try first the lightest load/heaviest gun combination, establish how this marries in with shooter stance and style and whether one can shoot a normal number of cartridges in comfort and, here's the rub, still break the usual number of targets or achieve one's normal average number of kills to cartridges on live quarry.

# 10
# *Problems of Master Eye*

TO enable the gun fitter-coach to produce a set of measurements to allow the gun maker/stocker to provide his client with a well-fitting gun which points exactly where the owner is looking it is essential to establish which, if any, of the client's eyes is the master one. Ideally the eye which is looking straight down and slightly over the barrel rib will be the master or dominant eye. If this is so, it will control gun point even if both of the shooter's eyes are kept wide open. Unfortunately things are not always so simple. Although most do have a dominant eye, this eye may not be on the same side as the shoulder pocket in which the gun is mounted. If the eye which is looking slightly down and over the barrel rib is the dominant eye, with practice these clients can soon shoot with both their eyes open. This has many advantages. Such binocular vision enables the shooter to judge range more correctly, also by using two eyes the peripheral vision is nearly twice as wide. On high driven targets the other eye can see round the barrel and assist in assessing any lead given to that target. Regardless of whether the shooter's dominant eye is left or right, if this dominant eye matches his right- or left-handedness there should be few problems for this fortunate person.

## TESTING FOR MASTER EYE

The textbooks are full of tricks like using a sheet of newspaper with a hole in the centre or a clay target with its middle knocked out. These are

***Easy to see which is the master eye*** *(Beamsley S.S.)*

***Using known empty and closed gun to check master eye*** *(Ladies Wood S.S.)*

unreliable and rarely used by a professional. The two most positive and easy methods to check for master eye are by means of a wooden dummy pistol with a front ring sight, or a known-to-be empty gun. The dummy pistol is given to the client who holds it in his front hand and points it at the coach's forefinger. The demonstrator in the photo to the left is the chief coach at Beamsley shooting school and the dummy pistol method is used extensively by him. It is very easy to see at a glance which eye is indeed the master.

***Wrong master eye, barrels canted***

## The Empty Gun Method

The coach takes a suitable and known-to-be-empty gun and, after showing the client the gun is empty, instructs the client to stand normally with his feet fairly close together with the body weight slightly on the left foot for a right-handed shooter. The client's arms will be folded which brings the right shoulder slightly forward to form a pocket. The coach closes the empty gun and carefully places the butt in the proper place in this shoulder pocket then places client's hands in the proper gun holding position. The coach stands some 6 ft in front of the gun muzzle and tells the client to keep both eyes open and point the gun at the tip of the coach's forefinger which is held just under the coach's right eye. If the client has a right master eye the gun should be pointing at the said forefinger. If a left master eye the muzzles will be pointing across to a spot

**Head tipped over to allow wrong master eye to look straight down and over barrel**

on the coach's right shoulder. When this happens, the client is told to close his left eye, and presto the muzzles will immediately switch over and point at the forefinger. This demonstrates to the client which eye is master. An exercise which takes less than one minute and does not blind the client with too much theory.

When the wrong eye is master the right-handed client will find his left eye is controlling gun point. Sometimes a young client will tip his head over the stock comb and use his left eye to control his muzzle point while still shooting off his right shoulder. In the USA some fitters will encourage this practice by supplying a straightish stocked gun which has had the top of the comb lowered to allow the head to be well tipped across and down.

The wrong eye is then centralized above the comb and looking straight down and slightly over the barrels. I believe this is a faulty technique.

The head being tipped over sideways, the neck muscles are always under stress, thereby resulting in recoil being more difficult to accept by the shooter. It is difficult enough to take the recoil from modern cartridges when shooting with the gun mounted correctly using the right eye and shooting from the right shoulder. Experience seems to prove that to tip the head sideways and down and use the wrong eye can result in strained neck muscles, a bruised face and gun headache.

## Central Vision

There are many whose eyes are of equal strength. If the client is told to mount and point the known empty and closed gun at the fitter's forefinger, this gun muzzle point will seem from the fitter's viewpoint to be controlled by the point of the client's nose. This is known as central vision. Guns can be stocked to enable those with central vision to shoot accurately with both eyes open. It is very difficult to measure accurately clients who require central vision guns and, even more difficult to produce such stocks. As a rule such guns can only be shot in comfort by their owner, and this only after many hours gun mounting and shooting practice. When their original owner no longer shoots these guns they are very difficult to sell. It is extremely rare that the gun will fit another person with central vision.

The majority of shooters with central vision can train their eye over the barrel to take control of muzzle point. This principle applies whether one is right- or left-handed. It is a matter of application and training consisting of slightly squinting the eye not looking down the barrel. This action in turn lets the barrel eye see more easily and so controls the barrel/muzzle point.

Many problems with master eye are magnified by the use of guns stocked with too low a stock comb which provides too much bend or drop. This allows the stock to be brought too high into the face and the controlling eye will be looking into the action strap and unable to see muzzles or target. When this occurs the other eye will be encouraged to take over the muzzle point, resulting in cross firing and missed targets. An experienced fitter will always make certain the comb height is high enough to prevent this happening.

## Wrong Master Eye

The right-handed shot will find his left eye is dominant and controlling his gun point. Left handers vice versa. Right handers who can shut their left eye, also left handers who can shut their right eye can if they so wish still shoot well from their normal shoulder simply by shutting their wrong or dominant eye as they mount their gun. There are many fine shots who do this. But by far the easiest method to overcome this problem is to practise shooting from the other shoulder. This will then be on the same side as the dominant eye, allowing this dominant eye to control the gun point. It is very easy for the majority of clients to learn to shoot off the wrong shoulder. So much is this so that the CPSA coaching committee encourage their coaches to learn to shoot off either shoulder. This technique enables them to demonstrate more effectively when coaching club members the finer points of stance, style, gun mounting and moving the muzzles out in front of the target.

## Examples from Experience

One of the finest shots ever in Great Britain is left-handed but has a right master eye. He taught himself to shoot from his right shoulder. In his competitive years he won nearly everything that was to be won. Another of our best shots has a left master eye and is right-handed. To overcome this problem he squinted his left eye and shot with a slightly higher comb than normal from his right shoulder. Again as a result of many hours of training he can now shoot with both eyes open from his right shoulder, but due to this training his right eye is now the master eye. Another coach is left-handed and has a strong left master eye. When coaching it was sometimes necessary to take and shoot a client's gun – most of these guns had right-hand cast – and demonstrate some facet of gun handling. Years of practice shooting from either shoulder eventually allowed him to control the eye looking down the barrel and make it dominant at will.

## THE CROSS-OVER STOCK

This allows a client to shoot off, say, the right shoulder and use his left eye to control muzzle point. Or vice versa. These stocks are prime examples of the gun fitter/stockers art, the stock being so shaped that although the gun stock is placed, say, in the right shoulder pocket the barrels are set way across so that the client's left eye is looking straight down and slightly over the barrel rib controlling muzzle point. These guns are usually made for mature shooters who have unfortunately lost the use of their right eye and still wish to shoot from their right shoulder. Those lefties who have lost their left eye can obtain left-handed cross-over stocks which work on the same principle.

I have known many who have had cross-over-stocked guns made and who shoot very well with such guns. A cheaper alternative is to learn to shoot off the other shoulder. Those who have unfortunately lost the sight of one eye are well advised to have a gun made and fitted to enable the gun to be shot from the other shoulder. Given the will and the application all those who so switch should eventually shoot as well as before. Some, who have been prepared to spend time on their dry mounting practice have found they shoot even better.

It is even more vital that the cross-over-stocked gun is a perfect fit; as with all guns it must be correctly mounted in that exact position where the fitter took his measurements and intended the butt to be placed. This gun mounting is not easy and it requires much more dry practice to become an expert mounter of one's cross-over-stocked gun.

Cross-over-stocked guns are usually very choosy regarding cartridges. Heavy load cartridges and sloppy gun mounting must be avoided if the client is to shoot accurately and in comfort.

Other disadvantages of these cross-over guns are that they are difficult to case and transport. Due to their structure they are easily damaged and when damaged are difficult to restock again. Some cross-over-stocked 'best' sidelock guns are even made with bent lock plates to allow the full amount of cross-over to be produced. These guns must be regarded as superb examples of best gun fitting, gun making and gun stocking. Owners of such guns should always be certain that their guns are accurately valued and insured. To restock these guns can cost hundreds of pounds more than normal restocking.

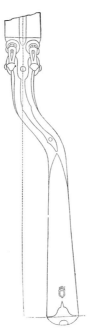

*Cross-over stock to allow shooting off the right shoulder while using the left eye (Greener, The Gun, 5th Ed, 1892)*

# 11
# More Eye Problems

## MECHANICAL AIDS

SOME sportsmen will have been unfortunate and lost the sight of their usual master eye and yet still wish to shoot from the same shoulder. Shooting school coaches, gun fitters and gun makers have long been aware of this. So, much ingenuity has gone into providing ways and means which will allow these people to shoot from their normal right or left shoulder and yet use their only eye which is situated on the other side of their face.

### The Monopeian Sight

One of the earliest examples of this was the Monopeian sight, described by Greener in his book *The Gun* of a century ago.

There are many who do not understand just how far adrift pattern placement will be when a gun is fired from, say, the right shoulder with muzzle point being controlled by the left eye.

There have been many in the past who found the fitting of the Monopeian sight did allow them to shoot competently while using their wrong eye. These sights do work and any competent gunsmith can make and fit them. There are snags however. The original outrigger front sight was usually brazed to the side of the barrel near the muzzles and was very vulnerable, being easily damaged or knocked out of alignment. As for the rear outrigger, experience has proved this is not required if the shooter

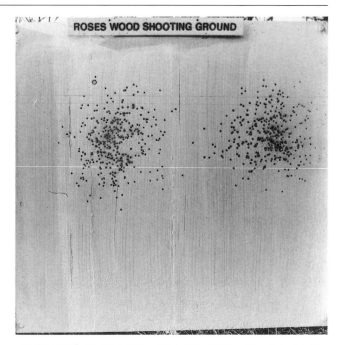

ROSES WOOD SHOOTING GROUND

*Pattern plate. The pattern to the right is the result of a right-handed shooter with a right master eye shooting a trap gun at a nominated mark. The pattern on the left of the plate is the result of a left master-eyed shooter aiming with both eyes open at the same mark. The left master eye controlled gun point and the target would have been missed by feet at a shooting distance of 25 yds*

*Monopeian sight (Greener, The Gun, 1892)*

has a stock made and fitted which correctly positions his wrong master eye to line up correctly the front outrigger sight with the target in such a manner that the pattern placement is accurate.

This modern version of Greener's Monopeian sight was designed by Clarrie Wilson and can be easily and cheaply made from 6 mm thick perspex sheet. A well-used favourite Beretta side by side model 424 was used for my original experiment. We cut a rectangular piece 90 mm × 35 mm from the 6 mm thick perspex sheet. A template of the outside shape of the gun muzzles was made. The perspex rectangle was then shaped as per illustration. This was done by means of a fine bladed hacksaw and files. The gun in question has a straight stock with no cast '-off' or '-on' so the outrigger sight was designed to be reversible. By removing the front sight and replacing this with a longer screw with the

***Wilson outrigger sight aligned with offset bead and left master eye***
*(Cheddar Valley G.C.)*

same size thread, the outrigger sight can be positioned either way to be used by a left- or right-handed shot. The outrigger portion has a series of holes drilled down through it which are 2.5 mm in diameter. The outrigger bead sight can be correctly positioned to suit facial contours and the width of eyes of the owner. For Mr Average the position of the sight was approximately 50 mm sideways from the original front bead sight placement.

This optimum position can be easily ascertained by experiment. First stand some 30 yds in front of a pattern plate. The gun is mounted on the normal shoulder. If this is the right shoulder, the outrigger wing should be positioned on the left side of the barrels. A small screw with a bead sight for a head is screwed in one of the holes in the outrigger and the gun carefully mounted and sighted as a rifle while pointing at an aiming mark on the pattern plate. If the shooter can call his shots this helps. If not the coach standing in attendance close behind will have to do this for him. Five shots should be fired, one after the other, and the resulting splodge on the plate will give one guidance as to how far across the sight is moved sideways along the outrigger arm. Once the exact position is finalized the arm can be trimmed to reduce its bulk.

These sights have been proved in practice. Ken Davies the chief instructor at Holland and Holland's famous school tells me he has had clients successfully using these sights.

## The Eye Corrector/Obliterator

This was originally designed by John Pesket of Cogswell and Harrison. They are at present available from A. Tucker Ltd, Gunsmiths, Chobham, Surrey in right or left hand models. The right-handed model has its obliterator patch on its left side to block out the sight of the muzzles by the shooter's left eye. The model for lefthanders has the obliterator on the right side.

There are many shooters who cannot shut an eye and others who feel inhibited when they do shut an eye. Others are concerned that one-eyed shooting restricts their field of vision which may result in taking dangerous shots. It must be agreed that to walk about with an eye closed is tiring and does restrict one's field of view. When coaching one is frequently standing behind clients who sometimes in the excitement of shooting forget to close an eye. This of course can cause cross firing if the person has a wrong master eye. The eye corrector overcomes this problem.

For correct fitting, it should be slid back far enough so that when the gun is mounted correctly the obliterator patch comes directly between the wrong eye and the gun muzzles. This prevents the wrong eye attempting to or actually taking charge of the gun muzzles point.

Both eyes can be kept fully open, providing normal two-eyed field of

*The Cogswell and Harrison obliterator in use, left. Note how the left eye cannot see the muzzles, this allows the right eye to take control of gun points (Spa S.S.)*

*Incorrect use of obliterator, right. The head has been lifted allowing the left eye to see over the top and take control. The muzzles are now being aligned with the left eye. This would cause similar cross firing to the left as above (Spa S.S.)*

view until just before the muzzles are placed on the target when the barrels are swung up interposing the obliterator between muzzles and the wrong eye. This is a gadget which works and is easily removed before the gun is cased or sleeved. The corrector doubles as a hand guard, keeping one's fingers off cold barrels in the winter or hot barrels in the summer.

## Variations of the Corrector

Churchill used to supply his own version of the corrector. This required the barrels of the gun to be fitted with a small clip. The hand guard corrector also had a small matching clip. When the guard was in position the clips married holding the corrector firmly in place.

*Rear view of obliterator in use on Beretta s/s shotgun*

## Mickey Mouse Eye Obliterator

This was available from Purdeys, but I believe is no longer available. It was in effect the obliterator patch fitted with a broad black elastic band; there was no hand guard used as such. This gadget slipped up the barrels until the obliterator was in the right place. Many found these worked extremely well. Again they were easy to slip on or off and allow the shooter to keep both eyes open at all times.

## The Thumbstall

As far as I am aware this was another Churchill idea to overcome the problems of a wrong master eye. The shooter fitted a large thumbstall over the thumb on his front hand. If the thumbstall was large enough and the front hand was carefully placed in such a position that the thumbstall obtruded between wrong eye and muzzles this also worked.

## The Flag-type Obliterator

This was also simple. A spring clip which was positioned near the barrel breech had a small metal flag fixed to a rod along the one side. This worked on the same principle as the other gadgets and was equally effective. It is up to each individual to establish what gadget is best for himself. The above can be modified to suit single-barrelled or o/u guns.

## Special Shooting Glasses

It is advised that for safety reasons all shooters should wear protective shooting glasses.

I have had a pair of Mitchell Yellows for thirty years, which are shatterproof. Also on dull days they seem to improve visual acuity. The lenses are also larger than one's normal spectacles. They are designed to sit higher on the shooter's nose thus ensuring the tops of the frames do not intrude and cut off one's all round vision.

These safety shooting glasses can be bought with lenses of many differing colours to suit either the colour of the targets or conditions of light. Being shatterproof they may save one from losing an eye through a ricocheting pellet, a branch whipping back into one's face when 'walking up' or broken clay target fragment. Certainly when shooting live quarry or clay targets – especially sporting or skeet – they are a must.

Those who always wear glasses should consult their optician, explaining just what they require in the way of size and shatterproofness of the lens. If the optician is not a shooting person, all one needs to do is to ask for frames similar to those worn by modern snooker players with large wrap-round shatterproof lenses.

## Use of Glasses to Help Master Eye Control

There are those with wrong master eyes who cannot shut their said wrong master eye. It is extremely simple to take a known empty closed gun, and with the help of a friend, mount the gun in the shoulder pocket, then have the friend place a small patch 1 × 1 cm square of adhesive tape exactly on the lens used by the wrong master eye. The position of this patch is established by trial and error. It is placed on the lens in such a position that the wrong master eye cannot see either muzzles or front sight. In effect it is serving the same purpose as the eye obliterator and works just as well.

Years ago some shooting instructors/gun fitters advised their clients to visit their oculist and have him supply a pair of special shooting glasses. The spectacles had a small frosted patch on one lens to make it more difficult for that shooter's wrong eye to take control. For those who had the fortitude to put up with a small patch on one lens this was fine. Other clients would have none of it and, although many did order spectacles as described above, when the crunch came the spectacles stayed put in their shooting jacket pockets. There they had no valid bearing on the shooter's performance.

# 12
# Barrels, Barrel Ribs

## BARRELS

YEARS ago the standard 12 bore game gun was made with $2\frac{1}{2}$ in chambers and then proofed for a $1\frac{1}{8}$ oz. shot load. The usual game cartridge was loaded with $1\frac{1}{8}$ oz. of shot. Due to the shortages during the First World War this game load was reduced to $1\frac{1}{16}$ oz., with some shots even using 1 oz. loads. All this with a small reduction in performance. These days more and more guns are imported, the majority of these guns in 12 bore being chambered and proofed to take $2\frac{3}{4}$ in cartridges. Some of the Italian makes are proofed at higher pressures to take the $2\frac{3}{4}$ in mini magnum cartridge. The growth and impact of modern competition clay target shooting has resulted in requests from competitors for loads with higher velocities and increased performances. This means the standard $1\frac{1}{8}$ oz. load of today may be designed to be shot in guns with $2\frac{3}{4}$ in chambers and proofed at higher pressures. The owners of the older type of British gun with $2\frac{1}{2}$ in chambers must not shoot such high performance cartridges through their guns. For all queries on shotgun safety and cartridge compatibility the prudent owner obtains expert advice from his friendly local gun shop. This advice will be readily obtainable and free for regular customers. When one considers that feeding unsuitable cartridges into a gun may result in burst barrels or perhaps even worse, any small charge incurred by non-regular customers will be money very well spent.

## Damascus Barrels

These will probably have been made more than half a century ago. Any layman should have such guns gauged and checked by an expert before any shooting takes place. It is better to err on the side of caution and refrain from shooting modern hot loads through such guns. Only an expert can advise on the condition of any gun and its fitness to be shot and only then after carefully examining and gauging the gun. Until an examination takes place, not even an expert can do more than hazard a guess if asked to pronounce on the safe condition of any gun and its suitability to digest any cartridge.

## Modern Barrels

In this country 'best' barrels are usually of chopper lump construction, each lump being an integral part of its parent barrel. During construction these lumps are so shaped that they fit closely together to eventually form the one combined projection which acts as the barrel lump. On other guns the lumps are dovetailed or otherwise fitted below and between the barrels at their breech ends. Then they are brazed in position. Another method which has been in use on the Continent for many years is the monoblock system, the Beretta factory having successfully used this method since 1903. The breech block is machined from a single mass of steel, the lumps again being integral. When the breech block has been prepared by boring to receive the tubes, it is heated to around 350°C and the barrels soldered in position. A well-tested form of construction which allows the best choice of suitable steel for either the breech block and/or the barrels.

## Single Barrel Guns

The true single barrel, together with the semi-automatic or pump gun, is normally fitted with barrels which have thicker walls than those used for double guns, this regardless of whether the doubles are of s/s construction or o/u. There are good reasons for this. The barrels on a double gun have to be lighter and thinner to produce a gun which is not too heavy to handle. Those who make 'best' guns have barrel makers who are artists in contouring their barrels to produce a gun which is finely balanced and seemingly eager to handle as the owner wishes.

## Barrel Length

There is, and always has been a great variation as to what is considered the best length of barrel. There are so many uses to which a shotgun is put. During the past century popular lengths have swung between 24 in and 32 in. Even now all barrel lengths have their devotees, most of whom naturally shoot best with guns which have the barrel length they favour. In the early days when black powder was used it was difficult to obtain maximum thrust from such powder when shooting barrels of, say, 24 in. The following criteria have to be well considered before an opinion can be given:

## Game/Rough Shooting and Wildfowling Guns

Taking game first, will the game be walked up or driven? To attempt to walk 15 miles and maybe fire 5 cartridges during a long day suggests the selection of a gun which can be carried all day without too much fatigue. The driven game shot who walks but little, and may even have a loader to carry his guns to each stand or firing point has only to decide what barrel length best suits him when he is shooting his guns. One has to equate the number of cartridges fired and the cumulative recoil to the actual weight of the gun and the physical effort in its smooth handling first through a long drive and then throughout a long day's driving. The shooting school can provide our driven game or any live quarry sportsman with the answers to these questions. The wildfowler may also walk many miles for a few shots, and these shots will be at high/long birds. Or he may be able to drive very close to a flight line or even do some hedgerow skulking with shots taken at close ranges. The same criteria may apply to the rough shooter. All these factors must be considered.

In an ideal world the most suitable gun will be well balanced and fitted to its owner, with barrel length and weight to match the owner's physical make-up allowing comfortable efficient shooting. This while using a compatible cartridge for the purpose in hand. The shooter who chooses heavy guns, long barrels and heavy shot loads will usually find such a combination is not a substitute for field craft, range judgement, or efficient owner performance. Until clean kills can be made at normal ranges – i.e. 25–30 yds – ultra heavy long range weapons with tight chokes and heavy loads should be avoided, the owner not being competent in their usage.

There are those who go to the other extreme and choose a super light gun with 25 in barrels. They then do one of two things: fuel the gun with heavy load cartridges so making the shooting of their first barrel a penance. Worse, due to barrel flip, their second shots will be even wilder and ineffectual, the only certain result being sore shoulders and gun headache. Others rightly select a light load cartridge then, although they shoot in comfort, due to poor range estimation they take birds too far out. This means missed, or worse, pricked birds.

Ideally, the gun should be purpose-designed-and-fitted, then taken by its owner to a shooting school where it can be shot at clay targets thrown at speeds and quantity to simulate the flight of the live quarry which one shoots at in the game season. This while wearing one's normal shooting clothes and in the helpful presence of the coach. One does not need to go as far as one client: a stickler for realism, he insisted on placing three standard building bricks in his game bag. He then walked and shot round the full length of the shooting ground while carrying this brick-filled game bag. Another client was a noted pigeon shot: he shot his pigeons while seated. He came to the school complete with a five-gallon drum. Pandering to the age of the coach, he also brought a spare drum for the coach to sit on. This worked well. As most coaches will appreciate, it is a back breaking task to stand in a crouched position while trying to coach a seated client.

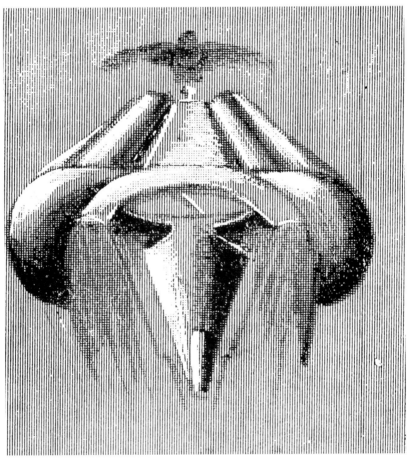

**Shooter's view down and over s/s barrels and top rib showing perspective** (*Experts on Guns and Shooting*, **1900**)

## Selection of Barrel Length in the Gun Shop

Mounting and swinging a gun on imaginary targets can produce misleading conclusions. This is similar to attempting cricket bat selection by playing imaginary strokes in the shop. One has to shoot clay targets or play real cricket to obtain true answers. The shooting coach is invaluable when a gun is being trial shot. He will assess its suitability as to performance. The would-be owner will find that his own body will provide him with the answers regarding how he can physically handle the gun, the recoil being felt and cumulative when shooting various brands and loads of cartridges. He should also take note whether he suffers gun headache more when shooting short barrels. There is more

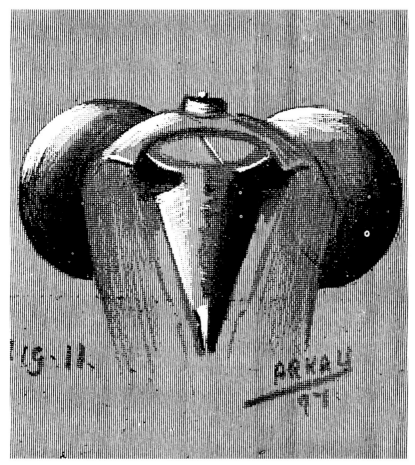

**Shooter's view over rib from a low combed gun stock. Note the greatly foreshortened perspective which makes accurate gun pointing more difficult** (*Experts on Guns and Shooting, 1900*)

muzzle blast from shorter barrels. Some, however, are prepared to wear some form of ear protection and shoot short barrels rather than shoot long barrels and use no protection. Armed with this knowledge and experience he should then be able to select a suitable gun with the length of barrels which best suits him and his chosen sport.

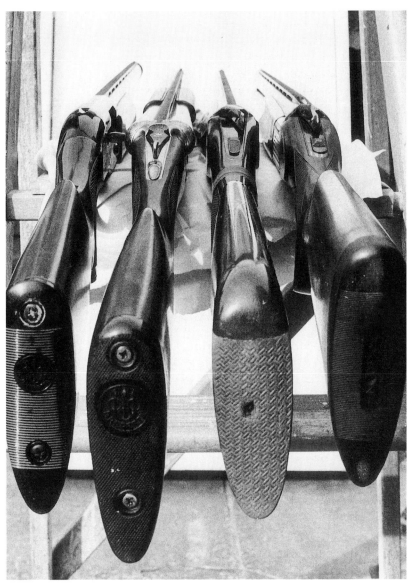

*A selection of four guns with anti-glare top surface ribs pointing towards the sun. Note how well the ribs show up, standing out against the barrels which are almost invisible*

# TOP RIBS

These may be raised, flat, swamped, of parallel width or tapering from breech to muzzle. There will be many who claim they never see their barrel rib. Very often this may be true, the reason being that they have never tried. There is no doubt at all that it is very easy for the majority to cultivate rib and muzzle placement awareness. This awareness can be achieved without taking one's eye(s) off the target. To refocus one's eyes back to and down on the rib or muzzles means taking the eye(s) off the target and results in a miss. But if the gun is fitted with the master eye looking slightly down and over the rib not only should that eye be aware of the rib and muzzles, but also such a perspective will allow the slightly foreshortened rib and muzzles to assist in alignment of target and muzzles. Too low a comb results in complete loss of perspective with the foresight apparently sat on the standing breech. Then there can be no rib-foresight awareness.

## Top Rib Surface and Width

The surface should be anti-glare, regardless of whether the gun is pointing into or away from the sun.

The raised rib with cross-milled top surface is fine and helps with rib-muzzle awareness. Possibly the American trap shooters have done most experiments on the many widths and heights of the top rib. The higher the rib above the barrel(s) the easier it is to see. Logically therefore the relationship of this rib and its influence on gun point should be greater. The high narrow tapering rib also allows the trap shooter to see the target more easily, read its line and know exactly the relationship between gun point and target at all times. If the targets are similar to the trap target and usually taken on the rise these high ribs in combination with a gun stocked to shoot high seem to help most shooters. The old-time live pigeon shooters favoured anti-glare ribs.

Some owners even go as far as to colour the top rib surface: one famous world champion Olympic trench shooter used to paint 1 mm at each side of the top rib yellow leaving him with an uncoloured centre strip. His answer to the reason for this painting was succinct: 'Well no matter what the light conditions are, I can at the least see something.' Others favour a broader rib with longitudinal central lines and cross-hatched edges. In most light conditions the cross-hatched edges show as shadows and assist one to be aware of the rib. In fact the sight picture resembles greatly what is seen by those using a double side by side in glare free light conditions. Others who have guns with this type of rib paint the central channel on the top rib with fluorescent red paint claiming that this produces an easy-to-see red line which apparently reaches way out to the target.

## Swamped Ribs

The smooth swamped rib so popular on side by side guns will produce most glare in practice. In fact to shoot a side by side gun with a swamped rib with a smooth top surface into the sun can be difficult. The barrels and rib are seemingly almost unseen against the sky.

Churchill did not favour the smooth swamped rib and designed his 'Churchill Narrow Raised Quick Sighting Rib'. This he fitted to his 25 in side by side guns. It has always seemed strange to this writer and many others that he so described this rib when at the same time he advised one should not be aware of the barrel rib. Be that as it may. For most shooters a top rib with an anti-glare surface which can easily be seen without looking for it seems to assist in knowing more accurately barrel-target relationship.

Many shooters do not always do what they think they do. The great American shooter Winans was a case in point. He always claimed that he shot running deer without making use of the sights on his rifle. He was one of the greatest exponents of this demanding form of shooting moving targets. To prove his point he removed the sights from his rifle. The result – a string of misses. He was then man enough to alter his beliefs. In fact he subsequently agreed he must have been using the rifle sights subconsciously.

## Ventilated Ribs

These lessen mirage/heat haze when many shots are fired quickly.

## Rib Width

This can be anything from 2 to 20 mm. Some find the wider rib an aid to prevent canting. Those who measure their birds and shoot maintained lead will find the wider rib gives them more lead on their targets. Others prefer the narrow rib believing this feature provides a more precise gun point.

# SIGHTS

## Front Sights

These come in many shapes, sizes and colours. The white bead sight set in a small tunnel so beloved of the American trap shot has much to commend it, showing black against the sun or white at other times. Although most claim they are never aware of their sights, they cannot shoot so well without them.

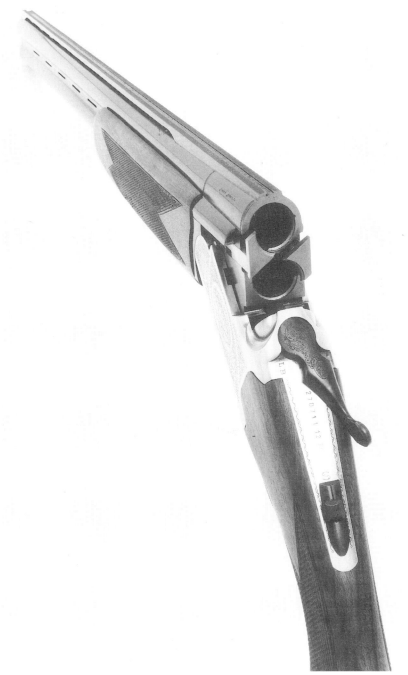

*Lanber gun with top rib with cross-hatched sides and centre groove. Some shooters paint the centre groove with red paint to act as an 'eye catcher'. This ensures that they 'will at the least see something'*

## Centre Intermediate Sights

These are helpful for dry mounting practice to check whether the gun is being canted.

If the gun is indeed canted the sights will be out of line along the barrels. The trap shot with his slightly high shooting gun soon finds out exactly what the sight picture should be when his gun mount is completed. Normally, and of course there will be exceptions, most trap shots have their guns fitted so that when the gun is mounted correctly the front sight seems to form an upside down figure-of-eight with the centre sight. Trap shooters will check this is indeed so when they have mounted their gun and before they call for their target.

# *CONCLUSIONS*

Each must obtain by practical experiment his or her own answers while trial shooting targets. Such practical tests should provide any thinking shooter with most, if not all, of the answers to the above questions. All that remains is the application thereof.

# 13

# Barrel Chokes

## HISTORY AND EVOLUTION

CHOKE has been defined as 'A constriction, usually at the muzzle end(s) of the barrel(s) intended to improve the density of the pellet/ patterns'. Discovered over a century ago, the extra range achieved by tightly-choked barrels was hailed by the pundits of those days as the ideal method for obtaining improved shotgun performance. Practical experience soon established that although the full choke boring of shotgun barrels certainly increased the killing range of that particular gun, the smaller area of pattern spread, especially at normal ranges, proved to be a greater disadvantage for the average shot. In fact for most types of live quarry shooting the tightly-bored gun possessed more disadvantages than advantages. The majority of live quarry targets being taken at 25 yds, improved cylinder boring with a standard load $1\frac{1}{8}$ oz. shot load was found to be adequate at distances up to 40 yds. Subject of course to the man behind the gun being competent and able to place his pellet pattern on to the bird. Even the expert shot found his full-choked barrels were placing far too many pellets in live quarry at normal ranges. This resulted in the shot game being unfit for anything but making into game soup.

Since that time, the ideal of a gun bored to suit each and every occasion, which was the unattainable dream of many gun owners, is now possible. Many and various have been the ideas put forward by gun makers to achieve this. To enable the widest variation in choke boring

**Full choke. Such patterns ruin game at close ranges**

and pellet pattern spread, it was first fashionable for a short time to order and have made guns with two or more pairs of barrels. One pair of barrels would be very open bored; these were used when the quarry was to be low-driven partridge. For decoying pigeons, shooting rabbits in close cover, widgeon in the moonlight, and close range clay targets, etc. the other pair of barrels were bored more tightly, usually being bored at least half choke in one barrel and full choke in the other. These tightly-bored barrels were used for the shooting of clay targets in the disciplines of Down the Line, Automatic Ball Trap and Olympic Trench. As for live shooting, some sportsmen used these tight bores for flight shooting pigeons, taking ultra high pheasants while standing at the bottom of deep valleys with the birds driven high overhead from the top of one hillside to the next.

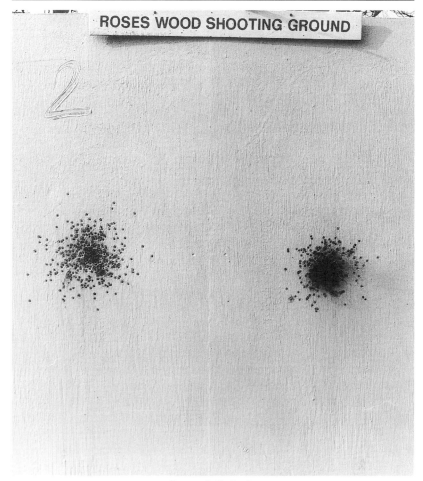

**Super full choke**

As soon as the gun trade established there was a ready market for different choke boring, gun makers began to consider easier methods of supplying the demand: the obvious answer being removable inter-changeable choke tubes which could be fitted easily and quickly to the muzzle ends of one's shotgun barrels. One of these early chokes capable of being attached to the muzzles was patented by Thomas Turner in 1887. This was a double detachable choked barrel extension and the gadget was fitted on the muzzles of side by side gun barrels and positioned there by means of a screw pin. This fitment is shown in *Practical Hints on Shooting 1887*. Its author claimed he had fired some one thousand plus shots through a double gun so fitted without the attachment working loose. Even in those days these fitments had to be first submitted to and pass proof, after which they were so stamped. The average weight of this double choke tube fitment was approximately 2 oz.

Between the two World Wars the Cutts compensator with its screw-on choke tubes became very popular. The compensator itself was in effect an expansion chamber with side slots fitted to the end of a shotgun barrel, the parent barrels usually being bored true cylinder. The choke tubes were supplied with constrictions which produced full choke, improved modified, half choke, improved cylinder and spreader type shot patterns. The Cutts spreader type tube became almost essential wear in the USA for the clay discipline of Skeet shooting. For DTL and similar disciplines the use of the compensator is not allowed because of the sideways muzzle blast being unwelcome to shooters standing either side of the compensator.

Years ago I carried out some experiments with Cutts tubes, even designing an oval tube which produced an oval pattern. This was similar in design to some of the choke tubes available in the USA. I found that, although in theory the oval pattern did help on targets which were travelling across the wider pattern of the oval, one lost out when the targets were travelling across the narrow part of the pattern.

Another type of adjustable choke which again has been successful is the collet type; this was claimed to provide one with the full range of choking at a twist of the wrist. Another improved type of collet choke was designed to tighten up one degree of choke each time the gun was fired. Both these collet types of chokes were fitted to single barrel semi-automatic or pump action guns.

Soon after the last war Greener manufactured sets of choke tubes for their Greener G.P. multichoke single-barrelled gun. These screwed into

**Winchester o/u with both types of Winchoke tubes, choke thread cleaner and choke removal tools**

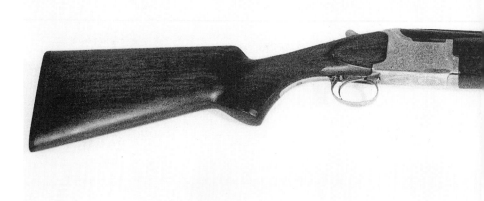

Winchester s/s barrels. Left with Winchoke tubes.
Right with integral chokes

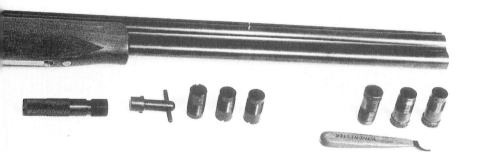

a compensator and although the patterns thrown were excellent, the blast from the compensator was unwelcome to anyone standing close by.

Since that time development has been rapid. Replaceable choke tubes which screw-on, screw-in, drop-in, add-on, are available in a wide variety of constrictions. Most of these tubes are superb examples of the gun maker's art, made of stainless steel, quickly interchangeable and allowing the owner to switch choke tubes in minutes. Equally important, the patterns thrown by most tubes relate to the constriction shown on the tube, i.e., if the tube shows a constriction of 20 points of choke, this should equate to half or modified choke, and usually produces good half choke patterns. The discerning gun owner can indeed select a choke which will almost exactly match his specific patterning requirements for almost any situation. Many new guns can be bought already fitted with inter-changeable choke tubes. In addition there are specialist manufacturers of custom-made choke tubes. Subject to there being enough thickness of metal at the muzzles of a gun it is possible to have one's own gun with integral chokes, bored out and screwed to take interchangeable chokes.

Another advantage of these interchangeable tubes is that today there are many who have come to live quarry shooting through clay target shooting. They favour the modern o/u game gun, but find the wider action barrel gape inhibits rapid loading especially of the bottom barrel when they are standing in a hot corner on a driven bird day. If their gun has a single selective trigger it is possible to place a suitable tube in either barrel which then enables the top barrel to be selected and fired first.

## CARE AND MAINTENANCE

Screw-in tubes are precision made to fine limits. After each day's shooting the tubes should be removed from the barrels and carefully cleaned, lightly lubricated and replaced. If left in the barrels they may eventually become rusted in. When this happens, either the tube or the barrel threads may be damaged. Modern tubes come in plastic containers and should never be stored loose in one's tool kit taking their chance with files, spanners, cleaning gear, etc. Should one mislay the tube case, it is easy to beg empty 35 mm plastic film containers in which one can keep the spare tubes.

To clean the threads inside the barrel muzzles some guns come with a thread chaser/cleaner. It makes sense to lubricate this tool lightly and run it down the full depth of the barrel threads each time the tubes have been removed. Guns with internally threaded muzzles should never be shot minus choke tubes. If this is done, the threads will become clogged with plastic or lead residue from either wadding or shot pellets. Those who wish to achieve the widest possible patterns can obtain screw-in tubes which are bored true cylinder.

*Showing sectioned barrels and screw-in chokes, Perazzi*

## CHOKE MARKINGS

There are many systems of marking choke tubes. Some use * stars, others O's, others * stars and – bars. A typical set of markings would be as follows:

\*       = Full choke.

\*\*       = Three-quarter choke or improved modified.

\*\*\*      = Half choke or modified.

\*\*\*\*     = Improved cylinder.

Although modern choke tubes are precision made, it must be stressed there is only one sure method to check the degree of choke constriction and the actual patterns thrown. This is by first ascertaining the average number of pellets in the shot charge for the cartridges on test. One must shoot at least ten cartridges in sequence at the plate, spotting and counting each pattern. One can then average the shot count of the patterns so produced and by means of Eley tables find the barrel choking.

# 14
# Triggernometry

## TRIGGERS

SHOTGUN trigger assemblies come in many forms. Trigger(s) come in many shapes and if not suitable can be reshaped by a gunsmith. Although the majority of the early double-barrelled guns, rifles, and pistols were provided with two triggers, even in those far off days there were a few double guns made with some form of single trigger which enabled the sportsman to fire both barrels while using this one trigger.

Side by side guns with double triggers are normally designed to allow the front right trigger to fire the right barrel and the rear left trigger the left barrel. As usual there were exceptions. When choke boring was invented some sportsmen had the right barrel bored tighter than the other which allowed them to fire this tighter bored barrel with the front trigger. This arrangement being eminently more suitable for the practice of driven game shooting which was then being adopted.

When the British o/u gun was re-invented before the First World War, most of these actions were designed to allow the top barrel to be fired first by the front trigger.

### Single Triggers

Mr Average cannot fire both barrels as quickly with a single trigger as he can when shooting double triggers. To operate a single trigger and fire both barrels requires the operator to first pull the trigger, then release it,

109

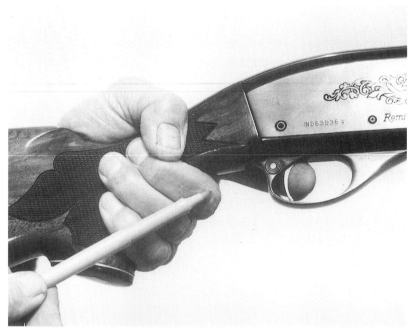

*Single trigger, correct finger placement. Note gap between guard and second finger*

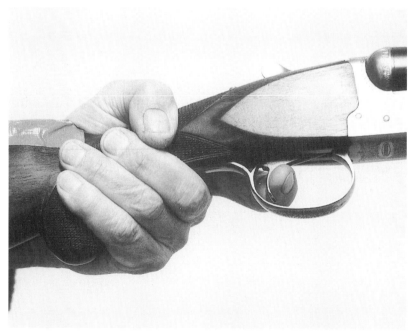

*Single trigger on a s/s gun placed well back in the guard*

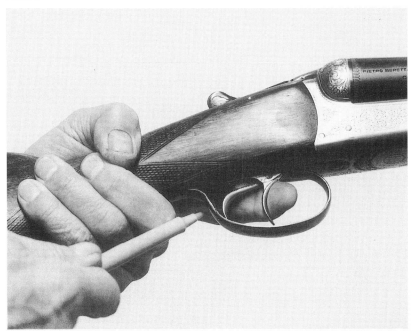

*Correct finger position using centre of pad. Note gap between second finger and guard*

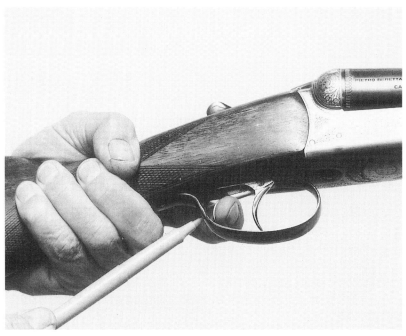

*Correct finger placement for rear trigger*

then pull it once more; a sequence requiring two movements rearward and one forward. When shooting double triggers the trigger finger can be quickly dragged rearwards with all movements of hand and finger towards the shooter. Correctly maintained, double triggers give little trouble; some single triggers, usually selective types, may not always function as they should.

The layman does not always realize triggers come in many shapes and sizes. Triggers may be placed in different positions inside the trigger guard depending on the design of the gun action. Double triggers may be set very close in line astern, or they may be designed with a gap between them of more than 1 in. Sportsmen with shorter than usual trigger fingers may experience bruising of their second finger on the trigger hand when shooting double triggers. Sometimes the second finger may be badly cut by the outside rear back curve of the trigger guard. This may be due to the trigger finger being too short to reach the front trigger unless the second finger is placed tightly against the trigger guard, or due to the finger being placed too far round the trigger. This can be cured by correct finger placement or, if due to a short finger, by buying a single trigger gun, the trigger of which is set well back in the trigger guard. This allows more room between second finger and guard.

Some modern single triggers are fitted to slides on the bottom of the trigger blade which allows a trigger adjustment inside the trigger guard of maybe $\frac{1}{4}$ in. Non adjustable single triggers can be redesigned by a gunsmith. The trigger is cut off at its base, repositioned and brazed back on in a rearward position to suit a short forefinger of a particular sportsman.

## Double Triggers

Double triggers on a gun with different choked barrels allow instant selection of the most suitable boring for the target presented, regardless of whether the gun is s/s or o/u. The seasoned live quarry shooter will select the appropriate trigger automatically without conscious thought. So much so that, on such occasions, myself and many others have been surprised on opening the gun to discover which barrel had been fired. The purist will argue there can only be one correct length of stock for a particular person. The double trigger action must provide its owner with two different stock lengths depending which trigger is being pulled. So, the stock length may be correct for the front trigger, the rear trigger, neither, or a compromise. Millions of first class sportsmen happily disprove these theories and shoot their double trigger guns with the same efficiency as those who favour single triggers. It is however easier to shoot single trigger guns when wearing gloves.

Occasionally one will have fired only the one barrel. With nothing else in view in the sky the experienced shot at once opens his gun to reload it.

The reasoning for this is simple: he has been taught never to be caught with a half-empty gun. At times, after the gun has been opened, the fired case ejected and before reloading can take place, there will suddenly appear another single bird in the sky. When using a gun with two triggers all that is required is to close the half-empty gun and pull the trigger for the unfired barrel. Simple, quick, and efficient.

## Shooting Single Triggers

When shooting a single trigger gun, the action of opening, ejecting a fired case and closing completes the cycle. The firing order of that single trigger gun will always return to its original setting. The single trigger being so programmed will, if pulled, attempt to shoot the same barrel as before first regardless whether that barrel is loaded or not. To pull the trigger releases the tumbler for the first empty barrel. If the single trigger is mechanical, one can then pull it a second time to fire quickly the second and loaded barrel. Inertia-operated single triggers cannot be so manipulated unless the gun butt is smartly hit to simulate the recoil required to operate the inertia block of the single trigger mechanism. The original Browning o/u and other guns of similar design, although fitted with an inertia block, can still be programmed to fire the second barrel even if the first barrel chamber has been left empty. To do this – after one has pulled the trigger releasing the tumbler and firing pin on to an empty chamber – the barrel selector safety slide is pulled back, then pushed forwards. The single trigger, when pulled, should then be able to fire the second barrel. Due to the fact that there are many many different types of single trigger now on the market the prudent gun owner must always check with his gunsmith to be certain that his technique for the safe working of single triggers, plus every facet of gun handling, is correct and safe at all times.

## Shooting Double Triggers

The stock hand and the position of the triggers should be a perfect fit to suit the shooter's hand and fingers. Ideally the middle of the pad on the front finger should be used to pull the first or front trigger. After this, if the stock fits, it should be possible to fire the second barrel without moving the trigger finger hand. The finger is placed slightly further through the guard while using the crack or first joint of the finger to pull the trigger. (See illustrations on pages 110–11.)

## Trigger Shape and Finger Placement

Triggers with a pronounced curve to position the finger positively are termed anatomical triggers. This can help to place the finger consistently in the same position on the trigger, subject to the stock grip being

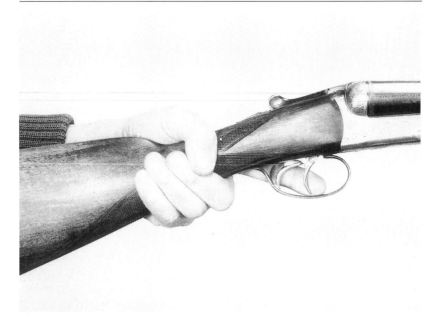

**Placing first finger pad sideways on the trigger will cause inconsistent trigger pressure and release**

correctly proportioned to match the shooter's hand. Poorly shaped triggers or incorrect finger placement can result in the trigger finger being placed along the side of the trigger. This alters the leverage of the trigger finger and the pressure required to release the sear.

Those unfortunates who are the unhappy possessors of the twitch or flinch should pay great attention to the shape of stock and their finger position. To operate a single trigger and fire two shots, the owner must pull the trigger rearward once, then release, then pull rearward once more. Due to the pressure of competition this sequence may be short circuited causing the pressure applied to fire the first barrel to be too light: the trigger may not move far enough to release the sear from bent. When this occurs, inevitably the shooter is leaning forward to take up the expected recoil. Due to the gun not firing there is no recoil, allowing the shooter's body to jerk forward with the barrels/muzzles flipping almost everywhere.

At other times after the single trigger has fired the first barrel, the trigger is not released. Unless and until this happens the second barrel cannot be fired.

It is essential that the trigger hand is positioned to enable the trigger finger to press directly rearwards. Allowing the trigger finger to push sideways on the trigger can cause varying trigger pressures. The stock hand should be fitted to the hand of the owner of the gun. The straight hand stock may allow, even encourage sloppy hand positioning. This in turn will cause poor erratic trigger finger placement and subsequent development of the twitch or flinch. Once acquired, I believe it remains to a greater or lesser degree for the rest of one's shooting life. There is no cure, although many have been tried. It is a mistake to have the trigger pulls lightened; this is but a short term palliative. All too soon the twitcher will report once more that 'the pulls seem to have gone hard'. There are those who have had their trigger pulls taken down to only a few ounces and who still cannot consistently release them.

## The Release Trigger

Although some world champions use these successfully this writer believes release triggers have no place in shooting. They are banned for some disciplines, although 'legit' for Olympic Trench Shooting. The release trigger works as follows: when a gun with a release trigger has been loaded the gun is mounted, the trigger pulled firmly and held just as firmly in this rearward position. Although this pulling of the trigger allows the sear to move out of bent, the tumbler is caught and held by a hook and the gun will not fire unless and until the pressure on the trigger is slackened. This allows the tumbler head to slide out of the restraining hook, fall and the barrel to fire. All fine in theory. In practice the writer has known those unfortunates who have the twitch to be unable even to release these release triggers. The only methods which may work are either to have the pulls made heavier, but short and crisp. The shooter *must* then really pull the trigger or he or she can switch to a gun with double triggers, each of which requires one positive pull rearwards to fire a barrel with no need to release.

## TRIGGER RELEASE PRACTICE AND TRAINING

From the time of the flintlock, thinking owners have spent hours practising gun mounting and trigger pulling. The old-time experts used hard wood inserts between the hammer jaws in the place of the flint. The live pigeon shooters of yester-year spent many an hour simply putting up their gun at various marks on wall or ceiling in their gun room.

One friend of mine had a large barn on whose walls and inside of the roof were painted pheasants and partridges in flight. Their lines of flight were also painted fore and aft of the birds. He had gone to great trouble to have the size of the birds equate to the size they appeared at the distances he hoped to shoot at them in the season. Some of these lines of flight were also on slow curves. When he mounted and swung on these pictures he tried to have his gun muzzles follow these curved lines. These days there are plenty of excellent snap caps which can be inserted into the barrel chambers to allow any one to carry out this gun-mount dry-firing practice. Split-second jerk-free trigger timing is essential for consistent shooting. Please do not use empty fired cartridge cases instead of snap caps. When the gun is opened these empty cases do look like the real live cartridge and muddles can happen.

Time spent on practising trigger release with snap caps on similar lines to the above has proved beneficial for most of us. Those who wish to delve further into the mysteries and importance of sweet jerk-free trigger pull and timing should read and study *Zen in the Art of Archery*. 'I have found when coaching that bowmen turned shooter understand very well the importance of sweet jerk-free release of their bow string.' In the book *Zen* the expert bowman practised his bow-string draw and release until 'when the sight picture required seemed correct the bow shot itself'; the string was sweetly jerk-free released without conscious thought and with perfect timing.

The DTL shooter will experience times when he sets himself up, calls for the target and when it appears there is no way that he can stop himself successfully shooting and breaking that target. Then he will begin to count targets, and bingo, one will fly away. Live quarry shots will often have had exactly the same experiences. Sweet precise jerk-free trigger release should be cultivated until it is as natural as breathing. In other words but a highly skilled craftsman using a well-loved tool. As an example of what can be achieved by this constant trigger-pulling practice I quote the example of one of the Russian champions. He informed me some years ago that he had fired many thousands of cartridges and acquired his 'muscle memory' by practising how to mount his gun accurately and smoothly pull the trigger, this before he ever fired a shot at a moving target. He was a superb shot and held world records. When on 'full song' he killed all his targets in the same place in their flight time after time. In other words his timing was always the same for each and every shot. This consistency allowed him to reduce the variables and achieve world records.

# 15

# Semi-Automatic and Pump Action Guns

## PERFORMANCE

THESE shotguns are usually not welcome at a formal game shoot, but BASC has estimated that there are at the present some 200,000 of these guns in Great Britain. They are used for rough shooting, wildfowling and clay target shooting. It is a pity that there are sportsmen who, usually due to prejudice and-or ignorance, wholly condemn their ownership or use, believing that the average semi-automatic pump gun owner is someone who always loads his gun with a full complement of maybe 4 shots in the magazine and one in the barrel chamber. To believe that the said owner always blasts off all five shots at a single bird is entirely erroneous as far as the great majority of the owners of these guns is concerned. Practical experience over the years proves these owners are just as responsible sportsmen and women as those who own and shoot other types of shotgun. The prejudiced will also claim that one cannot know whether a semi-automatic or pump in the hands of a nearby neighbour is loaded or not. This need not be so. The Bradley breech blocker is a fitment made of plastic which can be inserted in the breech. This fitment has a nose which fills the empty chamber and prevents a live cartridge being loaded into the barrel chamber and fired. This plastic plug is brightly coloured, thus allowing anyone with normal eyesight to see whether a nearby semi-automatic is loaded or not.

The one fault which does detract from the use of the semi-automatic pump on formal game shoots is the 'clickety click' noise made when an owner unloads his gun before crossing hedge or ditch. This could well disturb game which discounts the idea of anyone blasting away maybe five cartridges at one game bird. The Wildlife Act 1981 specifies that not more than a total of three cartridges may be loaded in a semi-automatic at any one time. To the best of this writer's knowledge there is no record of any prosecutions to date – 1988 – for disobeying this law. Regarding fire power, any skilled game shot complete with his trained loader and pair of fitted guns will shoot more cartridges on a hot stand in a given time than can a team of shooter and loader who elect to shoot a pair of plugged semi-automatic or pump guns. The great advantage in using a semi-automatic comes for those who due to arthritis or other physical problems are bothered by gun recoil. The semi-automatic scores here. The recoil produced is spread over a longer period of time, due to the breech bolt being driven rearwards, resulting in a long push being transmitted into the shooter's shoulder instead of a sharp blow.

## MAINTENANCE

Most new guns are supplied complete with an instruction manual. This *must* be carefully perused. Owners having any doubt concerning safe take-down or re-assembly *must* make use of the expertise available at the gun shop where the gun was bought.

*Breda semi-automatic gun with L to R, Breda manual, Bradley breech blocker, proof cert., choke removal key, spare choke tubes*

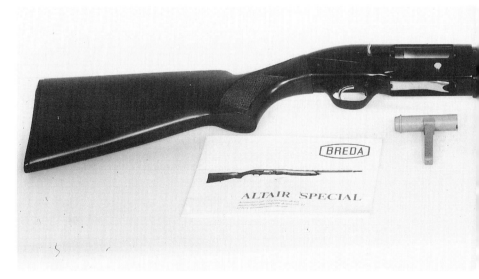

## Pre-Strip-Down Safety Precaution

It was a wise man who opined 'wasted precautions are never regretted'. *Always* physically and visually check that the barrel breech and the cartridge magazine is empty. The breech bolt movement must be controlled at all times. Bits of one's anatomy *must* be kept well clear and out of the receiver chamber and well away from the travel of the semi-automatic bolt, otherwise if the withdrawn bolt is accidentally released to move forward without hindrance one may lose part of a thumb or finger.

## After Take-Down

The barrel should be cleaned. Sportsmen should own at least four gun cleaning rods, allowing each rod to have its own implement left in situ.

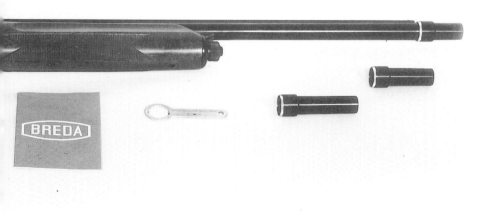

*This Beretta semi-automatic with its three interchangeable stocks and chokes is extremely versatile and can be used by right or left handers*

These implements are:

1. jag
2. phosphor bronze brush
3. bristle brush
4. wool mop

The writer prefers rods of full length, something to be considered when buying any new rod, especially to use on semi-automatics. The average semi-automatic barrel of 30 in length plus the barrel extension which fits into the action receiver will be usually at least 34 in in length over all. It is possible to buy rods of almost any length these days.

To use rods which are on the short side will inevitably put one's hands at risk. One method much favoured when rodding a barrel is first to always use long enough rods, push one of these rods together with its implement halfway down the barrel, then turn the barrel muzzles vertical. Holding the barrel with both hands press downwards until the receiver and the rod end sticking out is pressed tightly against the floor. This will push the rod through until the rod end complete with its implement comes out into the clear at the muzzle end. This technique keeps one's hands well clear of the receiver end, which very often has one or more sharpish projections, which can cause damage. The rod is pulled right out through and if further rodding is required the whole process is repeated.

## Gun-room Floor Protection

Inevitably the end of the gun barrels being cleaned become oily and resting them on one's gun-room floor will result in the appearance of oily ring marks. To make these blemishes on a nice carpet or parquet flooring is wrong. I, and many of my friends, keep an offcut piece of carpet on the gun-room floor; the barrel muzzles can be rested on this and the floor or carpet properly protected from blemish.

## Barrel Cleaning

A systematic method of cleaning a semi-automatic shotgun.

Make certain the gun is empty, both in the barrel chamber and in the magazine. Strip down for cleaning as per the instruction book. Remember when the breech bolt is in its rearward position in the receiver it is normally under pressure from the breech bolt return spring. It must be controlled.

The residue left after firing cartridges must be removed. There are many ways to do this. I have a rod permanently fitted with a well-worn phosphor-bronze brush. It is a simple matter to tear off a piece of $4 \times 2$ in flannelette, anoint it with Youngs 303 cleaner rust preventative or the like, place this patch over the old P/B brush in the shape of a top hat, rest the barrel muzzles on the offcut of carpet, and push rod, brush, and patch halfway down the barrel from the breech end. Take the barrel in both hands by the middle and reverse it and press the barrel down on the rod end. If one keeps pressure on the rod end long enough the brush end of the rod should pop out at the muzzles. One can then remove one hand from the barrel and pull the rod up and out at the muzzle end. This method does prevent one from damaging one's hands which can happen when one attempts to push the rod through with one hand on the butt end of the rod. Reverse the patch, re-anoint, place over the brush and repeat. This should have removed the loose fouling and odd powder flakes from the barrel. Take a rod fitted with a good quality P/B brush, anoint it with 303 and placing the muzzle on the offcut briskly rod up and down the barrel 5 to 6 times. Always end up by pushing the rod fully out of the end as described above. Then remove brush and rod. Again take the rod with the worn P/B brush, place another 4 × 2 in patch over the end and push straight through. Hold the barrel up to the light and 'view' it. To do this, let the light run up and down both inside and outside of the barrel.

Any leading of the barrel will show as darkish grey streaks running up the insides of the barrel. The worst places for leading are usually the chamber mouth and the choke ends of the barrels. Lighter coloured streaks, if any, are usually due to plastic wad residue. Skeet guns shooting small skeet size pellets will often lead very badly. This is due to small and very soft shot. Barrels which are chromed will usually clean more easily. Shooting many cartridges very quickly in hot weather encourages a build up of plastic and lead deposits. Energetic scrubbing with a good fitting P/B brush and plenty of 303 will usually remove the deposit fairly quickly. Obstinate deposits should be tackled by means of the heavy-duty Payne-Gallwey-type of P/B brush. Semi-automatic barrels have a gas bleed consisting of two holes; these bleed the gas from the barrel into the gas chamber underneath the barrel in which the operating piston resides. The bleed holes should be kept clean from fouling; if they are allowed to become partially or fully blocked the pressure of gas being bled will be reduced and this may cause an incomplete extraction and reloading cycle. The gas chamber should be well wiped with a 303 oiled patch and all residue removed. When gas chamber and barrel are pristine, a wool mop lightly dressed with 303 should be pushed straight through and out of the end of the barrel. Immediately before the next shooting session one must run a dry 4 × 2 in patch placed over the worn P/B brush down the barrel. This will remove any residue.

The outside of the barrel, especially under a ventilated rib – if any – should be well cleaned of dirt, water drops, and also blood spots which will quickly remove barrel blueing. When the outside of the barrel is spotlessly clean, a wipe with a cloth treated with Youngs 303 anti-rust fluid should protect it. The semi-automatic gas piston comes in many shapes and forms. Some are all metal; others have some kind of gas seal in the form of an O ring. It is imperative that this O ring is kept in good condition. Eventually due to wear the O ring will become damaged. When this occurs the gas pressure may be leaked and this will impair the ejection reloading cycle.

## The Trigger Mechanism

This is normally held in situ by means of one or more push-out cross pins. The Remington 1100 has two push-out cross pins whilst the Beretta 300 has only the one pin. It is worthwhile making for one's cleaning box pin pushers to match the pins in use. These can easily be made from silver steel rod and wooden file handles. The rod must be a snug fit in the action pin holes. It also helps if the rod has a slight taper ground at its tip. This allows one to marry up the trigger action on replacement, all of which facilitates pin removal and refit. To clean the trigger mechanism, a compressed air pipe is fine to blow out the dirt. Suitable lubricating oil applied as a spray will penetrate the assembly and keep it working sweetly. The breech bolt assembly should be controlled and removed as per the instruction book. It should be cleaned and treated in similar fashion to the trigger assembly.

The internals of the receiver/action must be cleaned, lightly oiled ready for re-assembly. The woodwork should be cleaned with a damp cloth, the checkering cleaned likewise with a toothbrush and then, depending on the type of finish, some suitable dressing applied.

## Re-assembling the Gun

The top of the bench should be clean and fresh sheets of newspaper laid down. Then all the parts which require lubrication should be lightly oiled and the gun re-assembled. After this has been done, the hands of the assembler should still be clean but very slightly oily. If indeed the hands are dirty or gritty so will be the parts just assembled.

## Storage

A well-aired cupboard is ideal. It is usual to store the gun butt downwards. If the parts of the gun have indeed been only *lightly* oiled all will be well. But if the gun's metal parts have been foolishly smothered in oil, this excess oil, which is normally a mineral oil, will drain down into the stock wood. The result being an oil rotten stock. Do not store guns in sleeve covers, it is essential to have the gun in a secure dry airy place.

Warning: Some gun owners are blessed with hands which perspire freely. This perspiration varies between individuals. Therefore the makers of 'best' guns, and indeed the great majority of gun shop

*Remington magnum semi-automatic gun*

*Winchester semi-automatic gun with Sorbothane special soft pad with rounded toe for a lady shooter*

*The young entry find the softer recoil of the semi-automatic much to their liking giving an improved performance when shooting a long competition (Urchfont G.C.)*

personnel and careful owners either keep a pair of oily cotton gloves or an oily cloth. Each and every time any gun is handled it must be wiped over with the oily cloth to remove all perspiration marks. If this is not done rusted finger and thumb prints appear within a couple of hours. If this happens it is usually impossible to remove these rusty prints without removing the barrel or action blueing. A correctly cleaned, lubricated and reassembled gun should, if stored in a secure well-aired dry safe place, only need careful examination about once a month.

The treatment of the magnum semi-automatic or pump is carried out in similar fashion. These big guns are very popular for wildfowling. There are some very responsible sportsmen who due to much careful practice on long targets at their usual shooting school are able to take their live quarry out to longer distances. In other words they do use heavy loads in a responsible fashion, usually loading one on the breech and one in the magazine. They do *not* shoot unplugged magazines. In fact there are many who always have their magazines plugged to allow only one cartridge to be loaded therein. The ladies and the younger entry do appreciate the softer recoil of the normal semi-automatic for clay target shooting, wildfowling and rough shooting. Even experienced, mature shooters have found that the use of the semi-automatic allows them to use full-weight clay shooting loads and still experience no trouble with excessive muzzle flip.

# 16
# The Side by Side Double Gun

## DEVELOPMENT

THE side by side shotgun was developed for game, wildfowl and live pigeon shooting in the latter half of the last century, and by 1900 this development had probably reached its zenith.

Right up to the onset of the First World War our great estates were vying with each other to see who could produce the biggest bags per day, and finally the grand total per estate for the whole season. The performance of the top shots was carefully monitored: many of these game shots spent most of their week days shooting game between August 12, the start of the grouse season, through to the end of the season on February 1st. During that period they were doing a ceaseless round of the big estates while shooting thousands of cartridges per week.

It is on record that the 2nd Marquis of Ripon shot half a million head of game in his shooting lifetime from 1867 to 1923. On some estates a grand total of 3000 head of game would be shot in one day by a team of 7 to 8 guns. Stanford, in his book *The Wandering Gun*, tells of one sportsman who took part in such a mammoth day's shooting on which 2929 grouse were shot; halfway through the last drive of the day this sportsman propped his gun up against the butt saying 'he was as sick as hell of seeing grouse'.

Shotguns which could take this huge amount of work day in day out and come back for more had to be well designed and superbly made of the very best materials. The rich sportsmen and women of those days

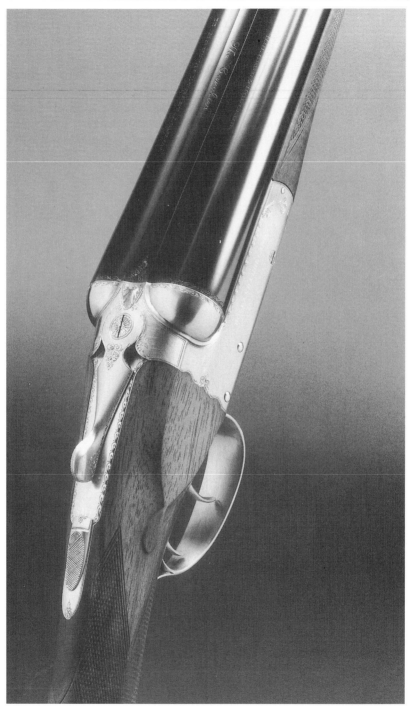

*Holland & Holland Cavalier boxlock hammerless ejector*

*Purdey s/s, sidelock easy opener hammerless ejector gun*

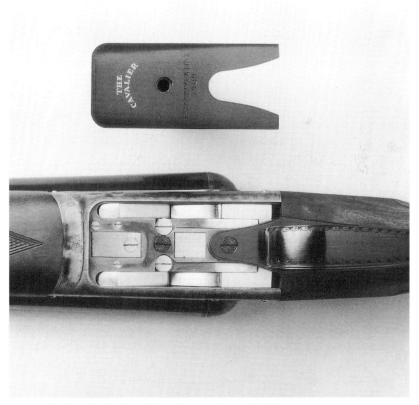

*Holland & Holland Cavalier, action with floor plate removed*

demanded the best there was available and were prepared to pay for it. Small wonder guns were developed to the nth degree. Most makers of 'best' guns regard this gun development as culminating with the sidelock hammerless easy-opening ejector side by side made to measure shotgun as available from 1880. Today's 'best' side by side guns are built to the same designs. Modern sportsmen will be surprised to learn that single triggers were readily available in 1900. Even so, in 1988, there are many game shots who still prefer to shoot double triggers. My old friend Gough Thomas once told me he believed if the single trigger had been standard fitting for those original double barrel shotguns, those gun designers who wished to make such doubles more versatile would have had to invent double triggers.

When used by an accomplished expert the double trigger is quicker to fire two shots than the single trigger. The double-trigger devotee pulls straight backwards with one long movement while pressing first the front trigger and then sliding his hand back on the rear trigger. Whereas the single-trigger user has to pull the single trigger to release one sear to fire one barrel, then the inertia block has to function and place the trigger blade under the second sear. While this is happening the trigger must be released by the shooter who then pulls the trigger a second time to fire his second barrel. The full sequence required to fire two barrels is pull, release, pull. Although the single-trigger shooter does not have to reposition his hand while firing two shots, the double trigger is slightly faster in the hands of the expert.

The owner of the double-trigger game gun with different chokes in each barrel has a quicker choice of chokes. Experience has taught him to automatically fire the barrel with the best choking for a particular bird. Driven game with a traditionally bored game gun will be taken by firing the left choked barrel first at the distant bird, leaving the right barrel with its more open boring to be fired next at a closer bird. When walking up, the right open barrel will be the first to be used for any closer rising birds, thus keeping the tighter choking of the second barrel to attempt the same bird if missed with the open barrel. If the first bird is killed with the first shot he will attempt a right and left and take another bird which will usually be further away from the shooter. Eventually he or she will practise this technique almost without conscious thought.

## Benefits of the Single Trigger

Those who suffer from cold hands can more easily use a pair of well-fitted shooting gloves when shooting a single trigger. When shooting double triggers often there is little space between the two triggers, which makes it difficult to use a finger covered with a glove. Those with a short trigger finger who find the back of the trigger guard causes bruising of the second finger of their trigger hand when shooting double triggers normally find this problem disappears when they switch to a single trigger; the reason for this being that the single trigger is normally set further rearwards in the trigger guard. This allows the trigger hand to be placed further back on the stock hand and makes for a bigger gap between the second finger and the rear of the guard. Some single triggers are placed on a slide. This allows one to move the trigger forward and backwards in the trigger guard to suit the shape of one's hand and the length of one's trigger finger. Assuming the owner is a safe and responsible person, he or she will be welcome without question with his or her side by side double gun on any type of live bird shooting. Suitably fuelled with the right ammunition they are as efficient as the person using them, maybe more so.

## MAINTENANCE

A well-made gun is almost everlasting if properly maintained by a yearly strip and clean at a good gunsmiths. All the lucky owner has to do is to clean and store his gun efficiently after use. The gun storage room should be at normal room temperature, well ventilated, dry and designed to give no easy access to the criminal. On their annual visit to the gun maker guns are stripped down to their component parts, each part being cleaned and polished with trigger pulls, action to barrel joint and ejectors checked and adjusted if and as required. The parts are then protectively greased and reassembled. This annual strip and clean should enable the gun to cope with being shot day after day for a normal season's work with no worry or malfunction.

### After Shoot Cleaning of the Double Gun

The equipment required for this is similar to that for the semi-automatic gun or any shotgun. (See chapter 16.) Briefly the main items required are rods, brushes, oils, powder solvents, gun grease, $4 \times 2$ in flannelette, paper towelling and hollow ground turnscrews.

Do not attempt to clean the barrel bores until the empty gun has been 'taken down'. This entails removing first the fore-end then the barrels. The gun is now in three parts: stock and action, barrels, fore-end. These parts are well wiped with squares of paper towelling to remove such debris as water and blood spots. The paper squares do this well, especially if slightly moistened with something of an anti-rust nature like Youngs 303 when cleaning the metal work. For the woodwork, which is also well wiped, the paper squares can be treated with a wood polish to marry with the finish already applied. Should there be grit or mud in the chequering, a toothbrush can be used to remove this and clean up the grooves. The fore-end requires the same treatment.

Old gun grease should be wiped off the action table, knuckle, slots,

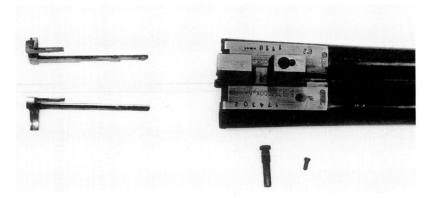

**Barrels with extractors, screw pin and locking screw pin removed**

standing breech, barrel lumps and flats, extractors and fore-end metalwork. Grease picks up grit in use, so old grit and grease must be removed. Then, especially if the gun has been used in wet weather, the stock and action should be well shaken. It is surprising how much water can be shaken out of the knuckle. The woodwork can be treated with a smidgen of stock dressing as advised by the gun maker. The stock hand should be inspected to be certain there is no indication of cracks or splitting.

The barrels must be wiped over with paper squares until clean and dry on the outside. Then the procedure for cleaning the bores is similar to that for any barrel which has been used to shoot modern cartridges: first the rod with the old p/b brush and its top hat 4 × 2 in patch. The patch will have been dressed with Youngs 303 solvent or its equivalent. The rods are always pushed halfway through, then the barrels turned end over end and pushed downwards breech-end first on to the hand end of the rod which has been placed on the floor. Gently push until the business end of the rod comes out at the muzzles.

If the rod is of normal length one should be able to take hold of the rod just below its brush and pull it out of the barrels. This procedure can be done easily even by young people: there is no danger of damaging the hand holding the rod against the ejectors; there is less wear and tear on the cleaning brushes. The same sequence of rods and their implements should be used as was advised for semi-automatic barrels until eventually all leading and plastic fouling has been removed and the bores are spotless.

The barrels are viewed to check for dents and bulges. When either is found it is unwise to shoot any cartridges through such a barrel. If the bulge or dent is not too severe, a gun maker can put down a bulge and raise a dent. He has the expertise and his advice should be followed religiously. To fail to do this may result in barrel or even owner damage. The extractors should be pulled out as far as possible; if much dirt is underneath, unscrew the extractor retaining pin and remove the extractors.

The valley on each side of the ribs should be cleaned with the edges of a folded paper square. Take an old feather or pipe cleaner and clean out the extractor leg holes, remove any debris under the extractors, lightly grease the cleaned extractors and replace. Make sure the retaining screw pin is fully replaced. If the pin head is left proud it is possible for it to be pressed tightly against the bottom plate on the action. To attempt further to close the gun can either push the barrels off the action face or bulge the bottom plate.

Boxlock actions annually stripped and cleaned should need no

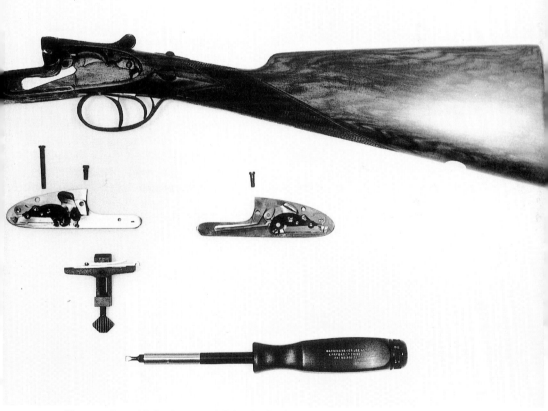

*Ugartechea sidelock gun with both sidelocks removed. Showing, centre left, **left sidelock with its mainspring also removed and cramped in a main spring clamp**, centre – **right sidelock**, bottom – **turnscrew with fitted hollow ground bit***

internal attention between strip and cleans. After wiping clean they should be slightly smeared with gun grease on joint, lumps, etc. Sidelock actions do make it almost too easy for one to remove the two sidelocks and see their internal state. To do this simple task all that is required is a well-fitting turnscrew to fit the lock-plate screws, *plus* the *gunsmithing knowledge.* The locks should be removed and replaced with great care and, as far as normal sidelocks are concerned, the locks are always at full cock when they are being removed or replaced. There should be no need for an owner to remove his sidelocks, but some will continue to do this regardless. To further dismantle a sidelock one requires a main spring clamp. This is easy to purchase at a good gun shop. It is less easy to obtain the knowledge on how to remove a sidelock and what to do when removed. All that should be needed is to smear the works lightly with a tiny amount of gun grease and reassemble. These locks are works of art and are best left to the experts. Regardless of the ease with which one can remove the locks on the sidelock, once these sidelocks have been removed it is strongly advised that the amateur leaves the remaining stripping down of the rest of any sidelock action or indeed the stripping down of the action of a boxlock to an expert. To take down either a boxlock or sidelock action is far from the simple job it appears. The writer has all too often seen the sorry result produced by the layman. Very often in the gun trade when one had customers bring in their own attempts at a strip and clean, this consisted of the gun being reduced to some of its component parts, with butchered screw-pins, scratched main springs, missing parts and so on.

It is part of the gunsmith's trade to strip down a shotgun. When doing this he has by means of years of long and hard-earned experience evolved his own time-saving techniques and expertise. For instance his vice will have proper protection on the jaws. This enables him to hold the action or whatever without producing scratches or other marks. He has his own selection of home-made turnscrew bits. He will happily grind any one of these bits to fit a particular screw-pin. In the unlikely event that he does not have a turnscrew bit to fit, he will make one. All of which takes time and costs money. *But* then when he does attempt to remove the pins he will do this with ease and efficiency.

There will be those, as is usual, who prefer to strip and clean their own guns. It is beyond the scope of this book to supply detailed instructions: far the best method is to purchase a good textbook such as *Amateur Gunsmithing* by Mills and Barnes. If this tome is studied and followed, the layman *should* be able to strip down his gun. I must however continue to stress that there are springs under pressure which can be easily dislodged and I can accept no responsibility for the consequences. Some have read the book and then successfully stripped down their gun; others have sadly – 'made a pig's ear of their attempts'.

The cleaning gear is similar to that used when cleaning any gun, i.e.

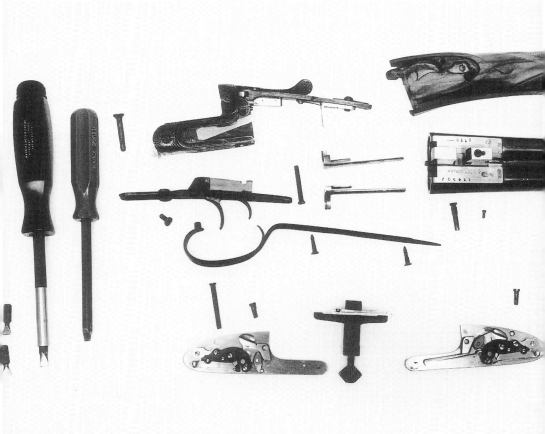

***Ugartechea sidelock action, partially stripped, with a main spring in a spring cramp. Gun makers' turnscrews and ground bits. The take-down of a gun action is best left to a gunsmith***

plenty of barrel rods. Correctly used for the purpose for which they are designed they are almost everlasting; some of the rods illustrated were made in the nineteenth century. Modern rods are even better being made of modern materials which are far stronger than wood.

Warning: do *not* wrap tow in excessive quantities around a jag, especially a brass jag. An over-tight brass and tow plug can be hammered through a barrel but it may cause great damage, even cause barrels to be reduced to scrap. Also do not spray oil in quantity – especially mineral gun oil – through each and every nook and cranny such as the front end of the knuckle and along the sides of the trigger slots. A well-maintained gun does not need this. Moreover oil swilling about inside the action will permeate into the woodwork of the stock hand which will eventually cause the woodwork to become oil rotten. When this finally happens a new and costly replacement stock is the only answer.

## STORAGE

After the gun has been cleaned, lightly greased where required and reassembled it should be handled only with the protection of an oily cloth; never the bare hands. Some even keep an old pair of cotton gloves which are themselves lightly oiled; these they don each time they handle a gun. All guns should be stored as previously advised in a secure place in a rack. Do not store in a sleeve cover or gun case as these may be slightly damp causing rapid rusting. Rusting will appear almost at once. When not in use inspect the gun at intervals of two to four weeks by means of an oily cloth or gloves. All depends on the thoroughness of the previous cleaning and preparation for storing.

# 17

# The Over and Under Double Gun

## DEVELOPMENT

ALTHOUGH many believe the o/u gun is but a 'Johnny-come-lately' this is not so. The 'stacked barrel' or 'superposed' as the Americans term such guns has been around for many years. British gun makers manufactured muzzle loading o/u guns. It is alleged that around 1900 makers of 'best' guns began looking around for something new as their 'best' side by side guns were lasting too long, being handed down from father to son, all of which made for decreasing sales of new guns. Boss had an advert before the First World War in which they depicted their 'best' o/u gun. One advantage claimed was 'the o/u gun pointed more precisely than the side by side double', the difference being that between pointing with two fingers – the side by side and pointing with the one finger – the o/u.

The majority of our top game shots stayed loyal to their classic side by side guns, although many of the makers of 'best' guns did produce their own version of the o/u gun; this was in limited quantities. Some of these guns had teething troubles; for instance, the bottom barrel was prone to misfiring. So much so that Beesley designed his o/u gun with an upside sidelock for the bottom barrel in an endeavour to produce a better striker blow. Ejection was also somewhat erratic in some models.

The American gun designer, John Moses Browning, produced his famous o/u in the 1920s. Clay shooting was going through a boom period at about the same time and the Browning o/u gun gave little trouble, was produced in quantity and at a price the masses could afford. It is interesting that most owners still use the term 'over and under'; this is due to the fact that the early guns were designed to shoot top barrel first, the barrels being bored more open for that top barrel. Nowadays, most double-trigger actions have their bottom barrels more open bored and the front trigger fires that bottom barrel first.

Single trigger actions which have non selective single triggers are also designed to shoot bottom barrel first. With the development of the selective single trigger and interchangeable screw-in choke tubes, owners of these guns can select the most suitable chokes for the targets thrown, and set the trigger to shoot first which barrel the owner wishes. The net result being most clay shooters first select the suitable choke tubes, then set the trigger to shoot lower barrel first. Except for the clay target flush competitions there is usually plenty of time between shots, and speed of reloading is immaterial.

The modern breed of game shot now coming in from the clay shooting fraternity is already used to shooting the o/u gun. Desirous to shoot some suitable version of the o/u on his live quarry he will often prefer a single selective trigger action with interchangeable choke tubes. This makes sense, being the most versatile. In fact it is the gun with all the options. After setting the choke tubes to suit the shooting to be attempted, the sst will be set to shoot top barrel first, it being slightly easier to load the top barrel than the bottom. Many times when shooting game the shooter will fire just the single shot; he has been taught never to be caught with a half-empty gun. Therefore as soon as he has shot his single bird the gun is brought down out off the shoulder, the action opened, case ejected and gun reloaded ready for anything.

## 'Overrun'

This can be a fault with some o/u shotguns. Whenever the gun is opened to its full extent – 'full gape' – and the front hand it taken off the barrels to reload, the action partially closes, reducing the gape. This reduction of gape makes it difficult if not impossible to reload the bottom barrel. This overrun is either a design or assembly fault. Very often it will not be in evidence when the gun is new and the action tight and often stiff to open. After a few month's use overrun may become evident. No-one should tolerate owning or shooting such a gun. The majority of guns open to 'full gape' and stay open. The faulty guns should be returned to the gun shop where bought with a request to have this overrun removed. If it is indeed proved to be a design fault the gun should be returned to the vendor as not being properly designed.

If it is an assembly fault, the usual cause is the cocking dogs have too much leverage and push the tumblers well back over centre. As and when the pressure of the owner's hand is taken off the barrels the mainsprings

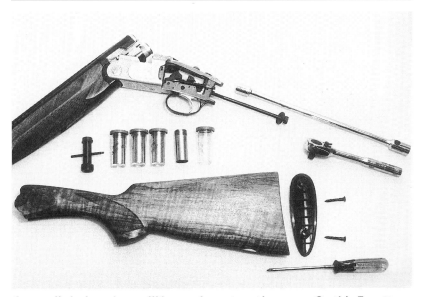

*Any well-designed o/u will have adequate action gape. On this Beretta as with most o/u guns the stock can be removed from the action in minutes by means of a socket spanner and a turnscrew*

exert pressure on the cocking dogs and attempt to close the barrels until such time as the sear noses fully bed home in their tumbler bents. Any good gunsmith can remedy this. Good gun shops have their own tame experts and will take the offending gun back and readjust. Some years ago there were a few imported guns designed and made with such a small gape that reloading was difficult. Such guns should not be bought.

## Gun Weight

It is possible to buy o/u guns whose balance and handling is very suitable for live quarry shooting. The prudent would-be owner will buy where he can try. Also they will patronise a gun shop competent to carry out any fitting alterations. There are many of these specialists about who will very often even carry out small alterations without charge when they are selling a gun. Even if they do not have their own shooting school they will have a tie up with a school which they know is efficient and who will do o/u try-gun fitting. There are many excellent shooting schools who not only have both s/s and o/u try-guns but are fully competent in their use.

*'O/U guns shoot high due to the stacked barrels being more rigid'*
Having met and fitted countless sportsmen and women for o/u, s/s, and semi-automatic guns the writer's experience indicates this is not so; other criteria such as balance, weight between the hands, trigger pulls, barrel length, etc. being equal. Experience has proved, at least to this writer,

that well-designed, well-made guns can be stocked to place their patterns exactly where their owners require. Trap guns with high combs will place their patterns higher than guns with lower combs. The only proviso being that all owners do mount their guns to position their gun stock butt in exactly that place in the shoulder pocket where the fitter intended.

*'O/U guns throw their top barrel patterns higher than their bottom barrel patterns'*
This is not usually so. It is true many DTL shooters do shoot over the top of their targets with their second barrel after missing with the first barrel. This is nearly always due to:

a Head lifting to see where the target is and if it has been killed. Mike Rose of the West London School aptly terms this 'bird watching'.

b Taking the second shot at missed target after it has passed the top of its trajectory and is beginning to drop.

Those who shoot a normal trap gun, set to shoot high. Where, for successful kills, the owner should seemingly sit the target on the front bead as he pulls the trigger and suddenly finds he is missing targets over the top must realize that the causes of the gun shooting high is as described above and due entirely to SF, i.e., 'shooter fault' and nothing else. It is simple enough to check where any gun places its patterns, all that is required is the use of a pattern plate and the ability to place the pattern accurately on the aiming mark. This latter ability is a rare achievement as far as Mr Average is concerned.

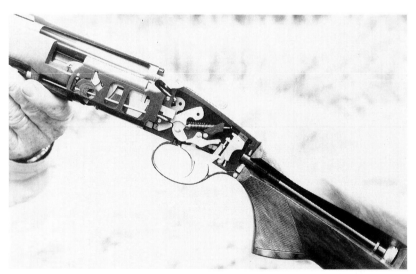

*This Perazzi o/u is shown sectioned to illustrate its internals. Note also the stock bolt. The head of this bolt has a hexagonal recess which allows the owner to remove the stock by means of the correct allen tool which is supplied with the gun by the makers*

*'Due to the stock bolt it is not possible to have the amount of "cast-off or-on" altered on O/U guns'*

This also is not true. Most o/us have a stock bolt to hold stock to action and stockers can and do use two methods to increase cast on o/us.

Method 1. They first remove the stock bolt, then slightly enlarge the hole through the stock for the stock bolt. They set the stock and action in a special clamp or jig and heat the stock hand – this used to be with hot oil. Nowadays many stockers prefer to use a couple of infra-red lamps for this purpose. New stocks with especially thick pistol grips may have to be heated and cramped more than once to achieve the required amount of cast.

Method 2. They remove the stock bolt and make another stud bolt which has a nut on instead of a fixed head. After heating and cramping the stock to obtain required cast, the stud bolt is bent to match this new amount of cast, the hole through the stock is slightly enlarged, the stud bolt screwed firmly into the rear of the action in such a manner that the bend of the stud bolt is in the same plane and degree of the new cast. The stock is replaced by sliding it down over the stud bolt, the new nut screwed down tightly on to the end of the stud bolt and all should be well.

## MAINTENANCE

Most o/us use a stock bolt to hold stock and action together. These stock bolts have either a slotted round head to take a screwdriver or a slotted hexagonal head to take screwdriver or socket spanner. The butt pad is removed and screwdriver or socket spanner inserted and the bolt removed. If the trigger guard is fixed to the action and has no retaining screws into the stock hand the stock can then be removed. It is easier to do this while the barrels are still on the action. All you need to do after bolt removal is to hold barrels and action with the one hand and lightly bump the stock heel with the other hand. This usually loosens the stock from the action. When the stock has been removed it is easy to lubricate lightly the boxlock works. Any other work should be left to a gunsmith.

Caution – when removing a round, slotted, headed stock bolt by means of a turnscrew, make certain the bit fits and is fully inserted in the screw slot. It is easy to place the bit down by the side of the screw head when this happens. An attempt to turn the bolt loose will cause the bit to exert pressure between the inside of the stock hole and the side of the stock bolt. The turnscrew blade may push out a sliver of wood from the stock thereby ruining it. To prevent this gunsmiths wrap a few dozen turns of plastic tape round the turnscrew half an inch from the end of the blade, thus centralizing the blade in the stock hole, preventing the bit sliding sideways between stock and bolt head.

## *CLEANING AND STORING*

This should be on the same lines as for the s/s gun with, depending on usage, an annual or bi-annual strip and clean by one's gunsmith with valuation for insurance at the same time. The day-to-day owner cleaning is similar to that advocated in previous chapters. There are a few points which should be noted. The knuckle joint often has a smaller bearing surface than that on the s/s. Gun grease must be used for joint and extractors after they have been cleaned of old grease, grit and debris. If a light oil is used for these parts, firing the gun will cause the oil to be bounced out. The parts of the knuckle joint will then tend to 'wring together' or 'pick up'. This requires gunsmith attention.

### Ventilated Side Ribs

Side ribs of o/us used to be solid. Now many popular guns have ventilated side ribs which help to keep the barrels cool. But in wet weather rain or mist can obtain entrance; a good spray of Youngs 303 or some other anti-rust helps to keep the interstices dry and rust free. Care must also be taken with the top rib; if ventilated these ribs can easily be dented by chance bumps or blows. To raise these is a job for a gunsmith.

### Storage

As for any gun. All guns must be securely protected against the attentions of the light fingered or foolhardy. The storage place should be dry and of normal living room temperature. The guns should be kept standing muzzles upwards in racks. Those who sluice large quantities of mineral oil through every available crevice in the gun's metalwork should desist. If they persist the surplus oil will drain down into the stock hand and it will become 'oil rotten'. When this happens the slightest bump on the stock or extra pressure will cause the stock to go 'snick'. The remedy is expensive – a new stock.

It is risky for the tyro to store his guns in take down cases or sleeve covers; there need only be the slightest amount of dampness in the case or sleeve cover and rusting may quickly begin. If not checked this can ruin a set of barrels within a few days. A lightly-oiled pair of cotton gloves or a cloth similarly treated should be used when putting guns into storage. It is true that gun shops can and do store customer's guns in box cases. However they are experts: their storage rooms are kept at the right temperature; they are also well aired and not damp. The guns in these storage rooms are inspected regularly by experienced staff who are competent and know how to prepare guns and store them safely.

# 18

# The 20 Bore Shotgun

## 20 BORE VERSUS 12 BORE

STUDENTS of guns and shooting will realize that for at least the past century there has been a resurgence of interest roughly every decade regarding the pros and cons of using a 20 bore instead of the standard 12 bore shotgun.

In this country the standard 20 bore game gun has $2\frac{1}{2}$ in chambers and the standard load cartridge has a shot load of $\frac{13}{16}$ oz. The standard 12 bore game gun has $2\frac{1}{2}$ in chambers and the usual load is $1\frac{1}{16}$ oz. To compare fairly like with like it is important to equate standard loads when comparing the effective performance of 12 or 20 bore guns. In America the majority of new shooters believe in 'getting there fastest with the mostest'. They have no proof laws as we know them in this country and the gun manufacturers do their own proof testing. To ensure these guns can take any heavy load cartridge their owners care to stuff into the chambers most American-made guns are built on the heavy side. Often being designed, chambered and manufacturer-tested to take the 3 in magnum cartridge with its load of $1\frac{1}{4}$ oz. of shot. These guns may weigh as much as $7\frac{1}{2}$ lb. To shoot these big Big Bertha 20s and subsequently claim one is 'only shooting a 20 bore gun' is to delude oneself. In reality these owners are shooting guns whose weights are equal to the heavy 12s, the shot loads being $1\frac{1}{4}$ oz. are also the equal of similar cartridges as made for a 12 bore by $2\frac{3}{4}$ in-chambered gun. The only fair comparison to equate like with like is to take the standard 12 bore game gun, with its

$2\frac{1}{2}$ in chambers and the usual $1\frac{1}{16}$ oz. shot load and compare its performance with the standard 20 bore with its $2\frac{1}{2}$ in chambers and its standard $\frac{13}{16}$ oz. shot load.

In shooting there is no action without reaction, and Greener's formula of a ratio of 96:1 gun to shot load weight of the standard cartridge for the same gun still holds good. For example a gun weighing 6 lb. equals 96 oz.; ideally this should be foddered with a 1 oz. load. The problem of mixing 12 and 20 bore cartridges is a very real one. To take a 20 bore cartridge and roll it into the chamber of a 12 bore barrel will seem an incredibly foolish action to any thinking sportsman. Yet it has been done. This live 20 bore cartridge will travel right down to the bottom of the chamber where the rim of the cartridge head will prevent that cartridge going any further down the bore. In that position some $2\frac{1}{2}$ in down the barrel that 20 bore cartridge cannot easily be seen. The unwary or careless may then too readily assume the barrel is unloaded. To then drop a 12 bore cartridge into the same chamber may seem to many to be even more foolish. Yet it has been done. When the unfortunate shooter fires the 12 bore cartridge the shot charge from that cartridge will fire the 20 bore cartridge sitting just below it at the end of the chamber. This double discharge can produce very high internal pressures with horrendous results. The gun barrel containing these two live cartridges of 12 and 20 will produce an obstruction burst just past the end of the chamber cone where the 20 bore cartridge was lodged.

When a barrel bursts in this manner, the sportsman may be lucky and only experience a severe fright and have a burst and wrecked gun to replace. Or, he may lose part of his hand, face, or his life due to this burst barrel. Many cartridge makers produce their 20 bore cartridges with a different coloured case to prevent gauges being mixed. The majority of careful owners also keep their cartridges well segregated and never ever carry mixed gauges in the same bag.

The unwary, the naive, and the inexperienced may well remark 'surely nobody, but nobody could be so stupid'. Here is a true story. A friend of the writer was paranoid about the problems of 12 and 20 bore shotguns and the possibility of mixing cartridges. So much so, he would not have any 20 bore cartridges in the house. He was also a keen cartridge collector, yet so strong were his feelings that he applied the same principles there. *No 20 bore cartridges* in his collection was his rule and he stuck to it. He and I were pigeon shooting one day. After about two hours' shooting the friend came across to my hide. He was white to the gills. 'I am not shooting any more today' he said; 'why', I asked. He then told me what had just happened. Comfortably esconced in his hide, he had had fairish sport. Then there was a lull, after which in came a pigeon. He pushed the safety catch forward and pulled the trigger which was a single selective. He heard the tumbler hit the striker but no cartridge was fired. As all pigeon shooters know, when shooting a single, selective trigger, if one opens the gun and ejects the empty case after shooting but one cartridge and then sees a pigeon approaching – it is very easy to quickly close the gun without reloading that barrel. The single trigger then returns to square one and when the trigger is again pulled the tumbler will fall on the striker on an empty chamber.

The real expert who is caught with a half unloaded gun simply closes his gun and moves the barrel selector to fire the loaded second barrel. Sadly there are few single selective trigger experts about. The majority of those with SST actions will, at sometime or other, have forgotten to reload their first barrel, and close the gun, then pull the trigger on an empty chamber. My friend believed this was in fact what he had done. He then opened the gun, saw a seemingly empty chamber and so dropped in a live cartridge. In came a pigeon, the gun was closed, mounted and the trigger pulled: the result – another click. On opening the gun the live cartridge is ejected. He picked up and examined the ejected cartridge. It was an obvious misfire, showing the usual signs of striker indentation on the percussion cap. For some unknown reason my friend then glanced – or tried to glance – down that barrel before he loaded another cartridge. The barrel was blocked. Mystified by this he took the gun apart. He cut a thin withy branch out of the hedgerow and pushed it down the barrel from the muzzle end. Out dropped a live 20 bore cartridge. He had never ever bought or shot anything but new 12 bore cartridges. The cartridge bag he used for his pigeon shooting was vast, it held over 200. He always tipped full boxes of 25 cartridges in at the one time. He had just bought a thousand new factory 12 bore cartridges. Somewhere among those thousand new 12 bore cartridges must have been a live 20 bore rogue cartridge.

In my own 70 years of shotgun shooting I have only once before come across a rogue cartridge in any batch of cartridges and this was of the same bore but with another brand name on the case. I have fired some half a million cartridges and handled many more when loading guns for clients and never ever seen a 20 bore cartridge in a batch of 12s. The odds against my friend having accidental possession, then unwittingly loading this 20 bore cartridge in a 12 bore shotgun must be astronomical. To then load another new 12 bore cartridge on top of the 20 was equally so. The odds for that new 12 bore live cartridge to misfire cannot be calculated. We decided he would never be killed by a shotgun accident: this was sadly true; it was a coronary some 10 years later.

There is something to be said for the old precaution that I was taught as a boy and still practise; this is always to blow down the barrel of one's gun immediately the empty fired case has been ejected. This blows out the burnt powder fumes, helps to keep the barrels cooler in a hot corner and one can *see* whether there is a wad or any obstruction in that barrel *before* inserting a fresh cartridge.

## MODERN CARTRIDGE PERFORMANCE

There is no doubt that over the past 25 years the performance of shotgun cartridges has greatly improved.

The majority of percussion caps are non-corrosive which makes for easier gun cleaning. Modern plastic wadding obturates more efficiently. The plastic shot cup protects the pellets on the outside of the shot column from abrasion as they travel up the barrel. This plastic wadding with its shot cup also tightens up the pellet pattern. This is due to lessened abrasion plus the concentrator effect of the cup as and when the cup and shot charge leave the barrel muzzles. The writer's own experiments over the past 30 years indicate that today many of our best-quality plastic wadded cartridges will throw between 5 to 10 per cent tighter patterns than either their modern fibre-wadded counterpart or the best felt-

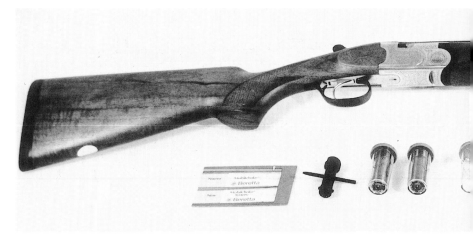

*Beretta 20 bore o/u **with interchangeable choke tubes***

wadded cartridges of yester-year. The advent of the pie crimp case closure, plus the abolition of the overshot card wad has eliminated cartwheel patterns. These tighter patterns mean many owners are shooting half-choke patterns instead of the more suitable improved cylinder patterns. Owners who find their guns seem to be producing 'overkill' should seek expert advice. By means of a gunsmith and pattern-plate testing at a shooting school one can establish exactly what patterns are being thrown by any combination of gun and cartridge. It is foolish for the tyro to gauge the muzzle constriction in an attempt to estimate the amount of choke and tightness of patterns. Such a ploy is a guesstimate, and often bears no resemblance to actual fact. If, when plated, a gun is found to be throwing tighter patterns than required, a barrel borer will soon open up the chokes, resulting in an improved spread of patterns and shooter performance.

## Comparing the Efficiency of Standard 12 and 20 Bore Loads

Pellets in the 30 in circle.

| Improved cylinder boring. | 25 yds | 30 yds | 35 yds | 40 yds |
|---|---|---|---|---|
| 12 bore $1\frac{1}{16}$ oz. $361 \times 7$ s | 296 | 259 | 216 | 180 |
| 20 bore $\frac{13}{16}$ oz. $276 \times 7$ s | 226 | 198 | 165 | 138 |

Live quarry birds are taken within a distance of 30 yds. This is 90 ft and it is a tallish tree which tops even 60 ft.

A century ago Payne-Gallwey demonstrated that a combination of ic boring of a $1\frac{1}{16}$ oz. load of 7 s (361 pellets) produced 50 per cent patterns at 40 yds in a 30 in diameter circle. His experiments proved this pattern produced a count of 180 pellets and was adequate to kill pheasants cleanly at 40 yds distance.

If this 12 bore load is classified as providing 100 per cent performance, comparison between the two loads show the 20 bore produces a 76 per cent performance compared with the 100 per cent of the 12 bore load. Practical experience has proved many times that Payne-Gallwey 180 pellet yardstick is correct so the 198 pellets thrown by the 20 bore at 30 yds is indeed ample if the operator is competent enough to place the pellets on the target.

Therefore the owner of the 12 bore with its $1\frac{1}{16}$ oz. load is really overgunned when taking his game at the normal 25 yds. This is the reason why the 1 oz. game load, such as the Eley Impax which provides 240 pellets in the 30 in circle is so popular and effective up to at least the 35 yds which is regarded as an extreme range shot by most sportsmen.

## Choice of Gun Weight

It is possible to buy extremely lightweight 20 bore guns, but, unless it is intended to shoot but few cartridges while walking long distances, the majority of sportsmen or women from the ages of 13 to 14 upwards will find the full weight 20 bore – say around 6 lb. – will soak up recoil and prove more comfortable to carry and shoot. Normally as always it will be the owner of the gun who will be the limiting factor as far as performance is concerned. Guns of this weight are not so whippy as ultra-light guns. Barrel lengths can be 26 in through to 30 in, with the 27–28 in being most popular; they handle and point well and, if well maintained, will find very ready buyers when they are finally sold.

# 19

# The 28 Bore Shotgun

## THE 28 BORE GUN

THE 28 bore gun is available as a single barrel, semi-automatic and also as a double gun of either superposed or s/s construction. The shot load is based on the bore which accepted a lead ball of equal diameter and which was 28 to the lb.

The standard British 28 bore cartridge for a $2\frac{1}{2}$ in diameter chambered gun has a $\frac{9}{16}$ oz. shot load. The majority of modern imported 28 bore shotguns will have $2\frac{3}{4}$ in chambers and take $\frac{11}{16}$ oz. loads. As always it is the responsibility of the shooter to obtain expert advice from his gun shop regarding what cartridge is suitable for any gun in his possession.

28 bore guns have been very popular for many years. In this country there are plenty of sporting families who have amongst their family treasures a s/s 28 bore gun. Such a gun may be possibly anything up to a hundred years old. It will have been carefully used for entry into shooting by the member(s) of each new generation as they come along. After such usage for a few years it will be again stripped, cleaned and carefully stored until some other youngster is to be entered to the sport. Within its limitations a 28 bore gun is a fine first tool with which any youngster can be taught safe gun handling and efficient shooting.

Although the shot load is small, it does contain enough shot to be effective on live quarry taken within a range of 25 yds. This range limitation does teach the young shot self discipline as far as effective ranges are concerned. The recoil will not be regarded as excessive by any

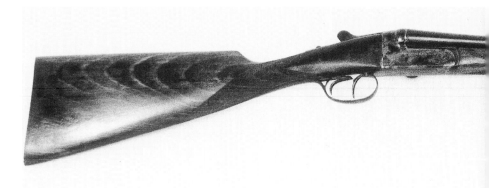

***Aya No 3. s/s 28 bore hammerless boxlock non-ejector***

well-grown youngster of 12 years or more of age. The gun weight should also be well within the physical capabilities of the young.

## Advantages and Disadvantages

It is not generally realized that there can be problems with using 20 and 28 bore shotguns in the same family. A 28 bore cartridge will drop into a 20 bore shotgun barrel chamber. When the rim of the cartridge head reaches the end of the chamber it will lodge there. It is then all too easy to drop a live 20 bore cartridge into that same chamber which has a live 28 cartridge wedged at the end of the seemingly empty chamber. Should the owner then close the gun and pull the trigger to fire that 20 bore the results can be as horrendous as those which occur when firing a 12 bore gun which has a 20 bore cartridge wedged at the end of the chamber. Therefore 20 and 28 bore cartridges must be kept segregated at all times.

The old English 28 bore guns when made as single barrel guns were often on the light side and the recoil excessive. Even the s/s doubles could also be so light that they too produced excessive recoil. This is further bedevilled due to the fact that many of these 28s will have been shortened as far as stock length is concerned at some time in the distant past. In theory when these guns have their stocks shortened the sawn-off piece of wood is carefully stored away until the youngster has grown and can take a longer stock. When this occurs the stored piece is retrieved and glued back on again. A 'best' English gun can be made to any weight and specification. As for the imported 28 bores these can be obtained in s/s or o/u conformation. For instance some importers are bringing in s/s 28s which have been carefully designed as scaled down replicas of the larger 20 and 12 bore models. These are available as hammerless or as hammerless ejectors, and in all grades up to 'best'.

The same principles apply to the o/u 28 bore guns which can be bought in all grades, some with interchangeable stocks. These stocks can

be swapped over very easily in about three minutes. All that is required is a turnscrew and stock bolt remover. There are some families who have bought a gun which has two stocks of different length. This allows members of the same family who are at different stages of growth to both shoot with the same gun in comfort. Moreover if the gun has 70 mm chambers the older youth can shoot the heavier load and the younger shoot the lighter load with less recoil. The gunsmith will advise.

## Choice of Boring

All too often 28 bore guns are supplied with half and full boring. It is more realistic to specify boring of improved cylinder and half choke. The young entry who is shooting the standard cartridge is taught to take his quarry within a reasonable distance of up to 25 yds. Game taken at such ranges will be killed cleanly enough if the sportsman plays his part and places the shot pattern on the front end of the bird.

## Clay Target Shooting

When shooting targets, any small chips off a shot-at target which is visible to the referee will be scored and count as well as those pulverized targets which have been smoked. The majority of the younger entries will find IC and half-choke boring adequate for most sporting types of target when shot at normal ranges.

The younger entry is more adaptable than the stiffer-jointed elderly sportsman or woman. These youngsters when 'shown how' can with practice both adapt and more easily fit themselves to the gun. Even so, it is well worthwhile making sure the gun is a reasonable fit. Correct comb height is probably the most vital; many times a youngster has been assessed as having a wrong master eye, when in fact too low a stock comb

*Too low a comb encourages the use of the wrong eye*

is the culprit; this results in the aiming eye looking directly into the top lever. This ensures the aiming eye can see precisely nothing of the target; the wrong eye having no such obstruction will happily take charge of gun point.

## Other Factors Affecting the Shooting of the Small Gauges

'Best' English guns in any gauge will be test fired, then stripped down and the high spots removed. This labour-consuming chore will be done again and again until the new gun can be opened smoothly and sweetly by its new youthful owner. All of this expert gunsmithing takes many hours and costs much money. The lower-priced imported guns are often very tight to open and close. When buying a new small bore gun, it is sensible to take the young entry into the gun shop and let him try to open and close a selection of small bores while loading and ejecting a pair of snap caps. The correct method to open and close a gun is shown in another portion of this book. If one finds by trial that a gun is too tight and stiff to open and close, the gunsmith can and will ease the fit and tolerances until the youthful and prospective owner can do this without a struggle.

Another source of trouble can be the thumb-piece belonging to the safety catch. Some of these are extremely stiff and impossible for a youngster to operate. Again it is easy to enlist the services of a gunsmith who will ease the safety slide until it can be moved to 'safe' or 'fire' by any youngster without difficulty.

## THE .410 CALIBRE GUN (please note 'calibre')

The .410 is actually the internal diameter in inches of the barrel bore at 9 in from the breech. The Americans dub the .410 shotgun the 'idiot stick' for good reason. This writer knows of more than one shooting school instructor who dislikes coaching anyone who is using a .410 shotgun.

It is a fact of life that most .410 guns are supplied and sold with full choke boring. The shot load for a $2\frac{1}{2}$ in-chambered .410 is only $\frac{7}{16}$ oz.; hence the tighter than normal choking. This writer prefers to coach with a .410 with no more than ic boring and place the youngster in a position where he has a chance to take the clay target well within range. One shooting school coach likened the pattern thrown by a full choked .410 as similar to the pattern 'thrown by a rifle bullet'. These tight patterns are disheartening to the shooter to say the least, and it is discouraging for any youth to attempt to shoot normal live quarry with such a gun. Those who doubt this should take note of how many mature sportsmen they see in the course of a full game season shooting with the .410 shotgun.

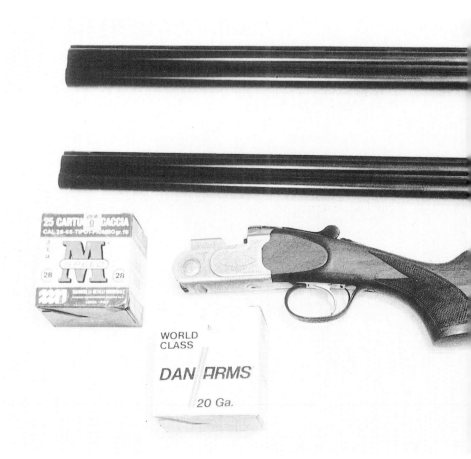

*A fine multi-purpose coaching outfit. An o/u Beretta 20 bore with interchangeable 28 bore barrels and stocks. One can also buy a Beretta 28 bore o/u with just the one stock and a pair of 28 bore barrels*

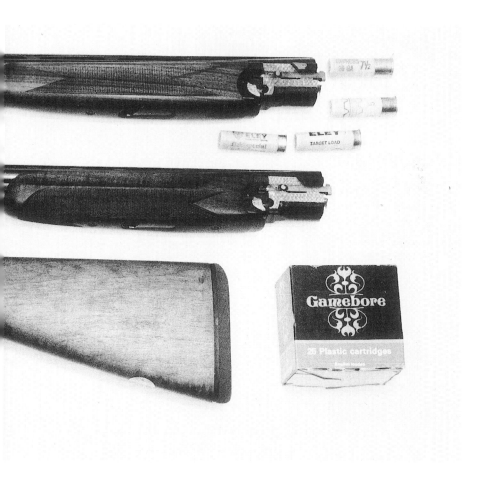

## *TO SUM UP*

For most sportsmen and women it is better to obtain a well-fitted 28 bore and take your targets or live quarry within range than to opt for the .410 with full choke and limited performance.

### Final Warning

There are still some 2 in-chambered .410 shotguns around. There are also unfortunately some 3 in-length cartridges. The proof pressures to which a 2 in-, or a $2\frac{1}{2}$ in-chambered gun is tested is $3\frac{1}{4}$ tons. For a 3 in case it is *5 tons*. Be warned and as aunts and uncles, *do not buy* a youngster unsuitable and highly dangerous cartridges. In the case of *any* doubt arrange for the gunsmith to gauge and check the gun before any cartridges are bought. For the rest, do the job of entry correctly. Buy the youngster a series of lessons at the local shooting school. He will enjoy these, deriving much profit, as will aunt or uncle footing the bill. The expression on any youngster's face as he breaks his first clay target is heart warming.

# 20
# The Try-Gun

## CONSTRUCTION AND USE

THE try-gun is basically a shotgun fitted with an articulated stock. This is normally 12 bore although other bore sizes have been made. It was traditional to have try-gun barrels bored full choke. Try-guns are usually designed to be capable of being fired. Guns of most types, such as single barrel, double barrel, either s/s or o/u, semi-automatic and pump have all in the past been fitted to act as try-guns with articulated stocks. The try-gun stock is articulated to enable the fitter to:

a  Move the stock vertically down or up to provide more or less bend or drop at comb and at the heel or bump.

b  Move the stock laterally to the right of the line of the barrel(s). This sideways movement to the right is termed 'cast-off'. Mostly required by those who shoot from their right shoulder.

c  Move the stock laterally to the left of the line of the barrel(s) to provide 'cast-on'. Mostly required for those who shoot from their left shoulder.

d  Extend or shorten the length of the stock.

e  Extend or shorten the heel of the stock, extend or shorten the toe of the stock. These two movements alter the 'pitch' or 'standout' of the gun.

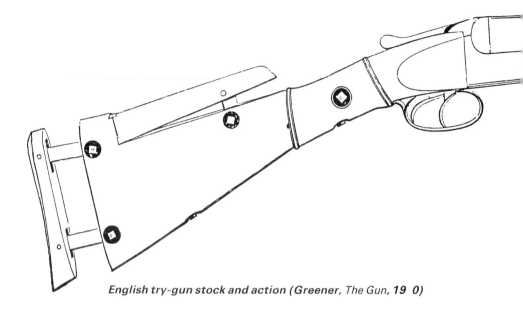

*English try-gun stock and action (Greener, The Gun, 19 0)*

Careful adjustments of some or all of these movements of the articulated try-gun stock may be required to produce a well-fitted gun which is comfortable to shoot.

## Producing a Fitted Gun by Means of the Try-gun

Both the fitter-coach and the shooter must work in unison until gun and owner are in harmony. The gun fitter's task is to produce a gun for his client which has a stock so shaped that when – *and only when* – the shooter has mounted his fitted gun in that exact position in his shoulder pocket where the fitter placed the gun butt and took his measurements, that client's eye will be looking straight down and slightly over the barrel rib. Such a fitted gun will feel almost like an extension of the shooter's front hand and arm. The shooter's front hand and the barrels/gun point will also be pointing exactly where the shooter is looking. If the gun does not so point, either the gun does not fit or the owner is mounting his gun incorrectly.

Due mostly to sloppy gun mounting or head lifting many do not obtain the best from their fitted gun, the butt being slam banged anywhere except in the exact position in the shoulder pocket where the butt was placed when the fitter took the required measurements. Clients who cannot be bothered to practise their gun mounting until it is 100 per cent accurately placed each and every time will never shoot consistently. The honest fitter should explain this fact of shooting to the client. Many who

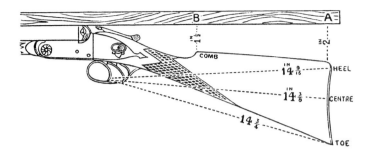

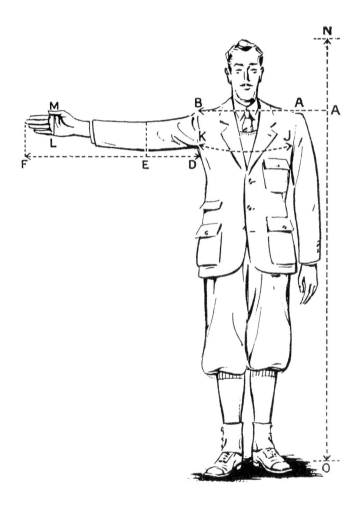

***Normal British stock measurements and where taken. With self-
measurement chart*** *(Courtesy W.&C. Scott Ltd)*

take up shooting late in life after they have made their pile are well capable of evaluating advice. Once they understand that successful shooting stems from client commitment they progress rapidly, becoming a credit to themselves and their fitter-coach. They also, as do most of us, derive more satisfaction from shooting well.

## Fitting Procedure

Each fitter has his or her pet methods. Moreover, given a reasonable chance, each will come up with a fitted gun to suit the client. Beginning with the novice, gun fitting has to be an ongoing process. It takes 12 months or so for most novices to achieve a suitable personal stance and style which makes for consistent gun mounting and pointing. Until this has been achieved the fitter has to assist his client to mount the gun correctly. In fact it is a realistic attitude to insist the client pre-mounts his gun when shooting sporting targets and having a gun fitting session during which time the fitter assists the client to place the gun butt in the correct position in the shoulder pocket. To allow the client to attempt to shoot targets beginning from the gun down position is a test of gun mounting and not gun fit. The measurements produced from such an exercise will be valueless.

## Testing for Master Eye

Ideally the aiming or master eye should be on the same side as the shoulder pocket where the butt is mounted. Thus a right-hander shooting off his right shoulder with a right master eye can shoot with both eyes open giving the advantage of wider peripheral vision and distance awareness. The fitted gun for clients with a right master eye allows this eye to look straight down and slightly over the barrel rib while shooting from their right shoulder with both eyes open. When hand, shoulder, and master eye are in unison fitting is straightforward. It is then usually a matter of stock length, cast, bend, and pitch.

The advised action to be taken when hand and eye are not in unison is for the fitter to consider the client, his age, character, and build. There are three courses which can be attempted. The determined type should try to shoot off the shoulder on the same side as his master eye. Concentrated dry-mounting practice for 5 to 10 minutes per day should work wonders in a few weeks, inducing muscle memory and muscle mastery. These determined characters soon make excellent shots. Those who insist on shooting from the opposite shoulder to their master eye have to establish their own technique which will allow the non master eye to control gun point. Control can be by mechanical methods, including glasses. (See chapters 10 and 11.) The alternative is for the shooter to close or slightly dim the master eye during gun mounting and firing. This

**Testing for master eye/gun fit. The Gun is** always first **shown to be** empty,
**Classic Double gun, A.J. Smith, World Champion, 1987**

*Demonstrating what the fitter-coach will see when a left-handed shot allows his wrong eye to take control. Note how the muzzle gun point is now lined up with the wrong eye, Classic Double gun, A.J. Smith*

*A good solid stance. Accurate gun mount with master eye looking straight down and slightly over the barrel rib, Classic Double gun, A.J. Smith*

*Using the bend stick to measure drop or bend at comb and heel*

dimming must always be done *before* that eye has had a chance to take charge and control gun point. Erratic eye closing at various times during gun mounting results in erratic shooting performances depending upon which eye is allowed to take charge of gun point.

## Use of the Corrector Type of Aid

Precise head placement with the cheek always in the same position on the stock comb is essential with an eye corrector. Head lifting allows the stronger eye to see over the aid and alter the gun point.

Should any or all of the foregoing fail the last resort is a 'cross over stock'. (See Chapter 10). But most shooters can, if they wish and will try, practise their gun mounting until they shoot from the shoulder on the same side as their master eye. Should they have lost their master eye late in their shooting career, they can soon learn with practice to shoot from the shoulder on the same side as their remaining eye.

## Stock Length

A long stock is difficult to mount. Too short a stock can allow recoil to cause the trigger hand fingers to bruise the face.

Much depends on a client's stance: an edge-on stance needs a longer stock. Once a particular stance has been developed, a stock length which provides a gap of between two and three fingers between the shooter's mouth, nose and trigger hand fingers will be found suitable for most people.

## Stock Pitch

This is an important part of gun fitting. Fitters specify a shape and angle of butt which matches the shoulder pocket contours and results in an even spread of recoil over the full surface of the butt face. The worst problems with stock pitch arise with those who are really well built, almost pear-shaped in fact. To provide a sharp-toed butt for such clients is wrong, the end result being that the recoil is transmitted from the gun into the shoulder pocket through approximately one square inch of the butt toe. This is uncomfortable. Even worse will be the effect of a sharp-toed butt on lady shots.

## Comb Height/Stock Bend

This is also important. If the comb height is too low the eye which should

*The gap between trigger hand, fingers, thumb, and shooter's nose, mouth, and face must be wide enough to prevent facial abuse by the trigger hand. Most fitters provide about a gap of three fingers' width, but much depends on the shooter's stance. Those with a square stance and style can usually shoot with a shorter length stock, the edge on stance requiring a longer stock to provide enough gap*

be looking straight down and slightly over the barrel rib will be doing no such thing. It will be looking into the bottom of the top lever and action strap. When this happens the aiming eye can not see the target; if then the client has both eyes open this low comb will encourage the wrong eye to take charge. There are unfortunately many such low-combed guns around and they should be avoided. Ideally for most live shooting and indeed as a good basis for clay shooting, until a client has acquired his own expertise for general shooting, either live quarry or sporting, the old game gun measurements of $1\frac{1}{2}$ in at comb and 2 in at heel are worth trying for a start. These allow a normally-built individual to sit the target on his muzzles and still shoot well. Most targets/quarry are rising and sportsmen shoot under these targets unless they head lift.

## Cast-off or -on

This is used to help the aiming eye look more easily down and over the barrel rib. Again much depends on any developed stance and style, the fitter using his expertise to determine the amount of cast required. There are also those who seem to be pointing their muzzles with the end of their noses. This is termed 'central vision'. More cast may help such people; if due to poor gun mounting or too low a combed gun it may not. No fitter produces measurements to act as a palliative for bad mounting. There are many excellent shooting schools at the present in this country. Most of these schools have try-guns, both s/s and/or o/u. Their expert fitter-coaches have the know-how to use these guns in a competent manner, eventually producing a gun which its owner can handle and shoot in comfort. Equally important, these fitted guns will point where the owner is looking. But only if that owner mounts the gun in the exact position in the shoulder pocket from which the fitter took his measurements.

No fitter-coach ever takes anything for granted. Experience having taught him that many clients do not do what they honestly believe they do. When asked the question, 'Do you close an eye when you fire the gun?' he will consider well for a minute and then reply 'I don't know.' Even those confident with their replies cannot always provide truthful answers. This is not deliberate as many do not do what they think they do. Some may close an eye on some birds only: one client shot with both eyes open on every target except the straight away, then he closed an eye. Although many experts will disagree with this technique, it worked well for him. One lady had a problem of inconsistency. There was no pattern of consistent behaviour to her shooting. The fitter found she sometimes closed one eye, sometimes the other on crossing targets. This regardless of which way the targets were travelling. Worse, when shooting incomers she closed both eyes. An eye-patch over the wrong eye proved successful.

For accurate gun fitting, plenty of time must be allocated. The client and fitter should be unruffled and able to give calm consideration to the problems arising. Wound-up clients and harassed fitters are unlikely to achieve success. Fitting the inexperienced person requires many visits to the school when he will also be learning much about gun handling and also the best methods of placing the pellets on the targets. Hence the need for a fitter-coach. There should be an ongoing development of a client's stance, style and technique, encouraging the client to work in sweet harmony with his fitted gun, which is after all just a tool.

The woodworking or engineering apprentice expects to spend five years or more learning to use his wood- or metalworking tools. The same criteria apply to learning how to handle sweetly a well-fitted gun. There is *no short cut*; *no magic potion*; no substitute for the hours of training which has enabled our top shots to achieve their exalted position. This is not *luck*.

To fit an experienced client also produces problems. It is comparatively easy to fit and teach someone to shoot who at first misses everything. Such a client is obviously doing something very wrong. The brilliant and erratic shot from one day to another can be a hard nut to crack, his problem often being one of attitude. The fitter-coach will try to calm such a person down and get him to 'call' his own shots. Unless one can do this it is impossible to know where one is shooting when on one's own. It must be very obvious that any client who does not know where he is missing the targets cannot correct his mistakes so easily.

There are many hard-headed businessmen who wish to shoot well; they readily spend much hard-earned cash to obtain a fitted 'best' gun which they will not take the time to learn to shoot. This attitude negates both the gun maker's and fitter's efforts and leads to the inefficient handling and shooting of superb guns. This is strange; they insist on trained people for their businesses, yet they never take the trouble to learn to shoot their fitted gun well. Very often this is due to the myth of the natural shot. Shooting is *not* a natural sport.

There is no such animal as 'a natural shot'. Anyone with normal coordination and eyesight can be taught to shoot safely and well if the will to succeed is present. The honest gun fitter-coach should explain these facts to his 'businessman' client. Once explained, businessmen will readily understand, alter their approach, and their shooting will improve. The above facts apply to both clay target and live quarry shooting, live quarry shooting being beset with most pitfalls. When shooting clay targets the club safety officers will see that the shooter is caged where required; they will also jump on any transgressor of the CPSA members' ten commandments of safe shooting.

The live quarry shooter has no such safeguards. He may be stood in a clearing in a wood, on the low side of a one-sided hedge. Also, although he should be, he may be unaware of the position of his fellow guns. If this is indeed so, he must find out quickly. *Even* then 'never shoot where you can't see'.

## TO SUM UP

The gun must fit, be mounted correctly and shot with confidence and understanding. A good fitter-coach will prescribe a set of gun handling exercises to enable the gun to be mounted in exactly the correct position each and every time, with the muzzles on the target quarry line. When the picture is right the pellets will impinge on the target and quarry in the correct place. Confidence will grow, shooting will be satisfying. All because the well-loved gun has been handled for enough hours until handled in style and complete harmony with its owner at all times. Hawker once wrote that he would prefer to see a sportsman miss in style. The experienced coach knows that once style has been achieved by the sportsman gun and owner will act in complete harmony. This unison will enhance and encourage both performance and enjoyment when shooting.

## SOME SUGGESTED CAUSES OF SHOOTING DISCOMFORTS

### Bruised mouth, nose or face

Stock too short, too loose a grip, head lifting, too thin a stock hand, slamming the comb into the cheek. Tilting the head forward so that the front edge of the cheek bone receives the recoil. Too much bend. Narrow comb. Wrong pitch or stand out. Heavy load cartridges.

### Bruised shoulder

Too heavy a load, too light a gun. Wrong-shaped butt with sharp toe and/or sharp edges. Loose gun hold.

### Bruised arm biceps

Sloppy or incompetent gun mounting, ill-fitting gun. Poor stance.

### Bruised second finger

Too short a stock, loose grip, too thin a stock hand, poorly shaped trigger guard. Trigger too far forward in the trigger guard bow. First finger wrongly placed on the trigger, too short a trigger finger.

### Gun headache

Too heavy a load, too light a gun. Usual ratio for gun to shot charge weight is 96 to 1. Powder fume inhalation. No ear protection.

## Frozen shoulder of the front arm

Too heavy a gun or too much forward weight.

## Flinching

Over shooting, especially with no ear protection. Too heavy a load, too light a gun. Poor gun fit. Over concentration. Too light a trigger pull, dragging and tentative trigger pulls.

Churchill's formula for pattern placement and gun fit is: stand and shoot 16 yards away from a pattern plate. For each inch the pattern is off centre another $\frac{1}{16}$ in of drop or cast is required to compensate.

# 21
# Modern Clay Shooting

THE number of clay targets shot in this country is now over one million targets per week and still rising. There can be few sports which have grown or are growing faster than modern clay target shooting. Except for the problem of noise pollution it would seem that the sky is the limit as far as the expansion of this sport is concerned. Clay clubs and shooting schools are proliferating rapidly. The CPSA membership increases every week. Not so long ago the total membership was in the hundreds, now it is approaching the twenty thousand mark. The number of clay clubs has also increased and it will be possible for anyone interested to find clubs within twenty miles of home. The enthusiast can shoot targets almost every day of the week if he wishes.

## WHY SHOOT CLAY TARGETS?

The ideal answer, which I am given many times, is 'to learn to handle a gun safely and competently'. There are others. Some shoot clay targets only. They are dedicated to one chosen discipline and shoot nothing else. These people are usually top-flight shots and keep their position at the high end of the CPSA averages by means of hard work, many hours of shooting among those with similar ideas, plus the expenditure of much time and money.

Others will shoot a mix of various disciplines. If they have a spell of poor shooting in one discipline they tend to drop that and shoot more of another discipline. Others are not competition-minded. They simply shoot targets for fun and prefer the informality of what they term 'the fun squads'. They do try to break their targets, but if they miss the odd target it is not the traumatic experience it is for the specialist competitor who travels the world competing at the highest level.

## The Skeet Discipline

The Skeet discipline was brought into this country in the 1920s. It was hailed by the pundits as a gun game for a game gun. Indeed as the layouts were designed then most of the targets were close and quick. The gun position on call for the target was 'down'. Most of the guns used were indeed game guns. The wise boys soon noticed that the open-bored guns helped to improve scores, also that the light game gun produced lots of recoil when used with the standard $1\frac{1}{8}$ oz. cartridge. So the semi-automatic gun with the Cutts compensator and a spreader tube became the essential weapon. When the Browning o/u and other guns of similar design were produced it was not long before these guns were available with barrel lengths from 26–32 in. The average weight of such guns was around $7\frac{1}{2}$ lb., all of which rang the knell of the game gun being used by the competitive types.

When the first isu skeet layouts became available in this country, many switched to this new discipline from the English-type skeet which they had been shooting. The gun position was 'down', and the rule wording was specific. The targets travelled faster and further and the guns became more specialized to enable these targets to be taken more efficiently. Those who shot for fun gave isu skeet a try but soon left it for less demanding targets.

## The Down the Line Discipline

The Down the Line discipline goes back a century and although it can be shot with almost any gun, a slightly high shooting gun with a fair amount of choke does help. Certainly the owner of the light game gun will find that shooting 100 targets with his light gun can be more punishing than he wishes.

## The Olympic Trench Discipline

This is even more demanding and requires the ultimate in specialist guns, usually of full weight and with 30–32 in barrels. Trench shooters are loners and o/t is a religion to them.

## Sporting

This comes in many guises. Originally the targets were thrown distances of 40–50 yds on set trajectories which were alleged to simulate the flight of a particular sporting bird. For instance the 'springing teal' type of target was a rising target which climbed to upwards of 60 ft. The shooter had to shoot at and kill the said target before it reached the apex of its flight. Modern high-performance traps throw targets much further – up to 160 yds. The modern springing teal target travels outwards and upwards to a height of maybe 120 feet at a higher rate of climb than ever attained by the live springing teal. To call such a target 'springing teal' is a misnomer. To help a little the rules have been changed and at present the shooter can take sporting targets at any time during their flight as long as it is safe to shoot.

## *SEEKING PROFESSIONAL ADVICE*

Those who wish to specialize in a particular discipline should as always visit the local gun shop and arrange to trial shoot that particular discipline at the nearest gun club in the presence of the gun shop coach. At the same time he should arrange to trial shoot the gun of his choice from that same gun shop. This may be done with or without the assistance of a try-gun. There are few try-guns for the trench disciplines; very often the fitter-coach from the shop can find a gun among his stock which fits near enough to enable trial shooting to take place.

Whichever discipline is shot, if the new boy is a complete novice he will first be shown and thrown straightforward targets on simple trajectories. A few words of warning: an expert gun fitter-coach to whom time is money has enough expertise to *set up* the client and will soon have him hitting about 75 per cent of these straightforward targets. When this happens our novice may well be mystified by this performance. Worse still he may mistakenly believe that he and the gun he is trying will in competition prove to be a world-beating combination. Sadly this is rarely so. The expert coach can and will set his clients up to shoot almost any type of target efficiently, especially when shooting selected targets in peace and quiet with no competition pressures or other distractions. In these conditions clay shooting seems all too easy. What a coach cannot do is to give the client the intestinal fortitude which allows him to break and keep breaking each and every specific clay target until he has 'straighted' a competition.

As well as the above who only shoot clay targets there are a great number of sportsmen and women who rely on their clay target shooting to hone their subsequent performances when shooting live quarry. They take the attitude that to spend hundreds of pounds on a day's live shooting and then shoot badly is a waste of time and money. They buy a season ticket at a friendly shooting school and usually hunt in pairs. The writer knows many who will meet a friend once per week all through the close season and have a couple of hours' practice on sporting targets. They soon get to know the coach and he them. Each and every time they shoot the coach will be pushing them to the limits of their competence. Known problem targets will be thrown, the results of the shooting analysed and remedial action taken. All of which produces the three Cs so essential to consistent effective shooting. These are confidence in one's gun, confidence in one's cartridges and most important confidence in one's self. These people are always 'shot in'. Due to handling their guns weekly they have acquired muscle memory; as soon as a target is thrown, the appropriate muscles are brought into play, the target read, and the shot fired. Usually successfully.

These sportsmen, who are really live quarry shooters wishing to raise their game as far as live shooting is concerned, are often worried when they first commence clay shooting. They will have been told by the old-timers that clay target shooting is no good for the live shooter. 'The targets soon slow down and all one does is to wait for them to do this; then they are easy to shoot and very unlike live birds who accelerate and usually do not slow down until they are out of range.' Years ago this belief was based on fact. These days with modern traps throwing midi targets 150 yds, this is not true. The flights of live birds can indeed be simulated, the targets so presented to the game shot that they are even more difficult than the real thing.

There is also the clay target flush. Here more than one trap will be used, sometimes even a battery of 6–8 traps, set at differing angles and speeds. The game shooters are spaced out in line as when game shooting. In some instances loaders are allowed. The guns made up in various teams, the resulting stream of targets thrown allows the gun and his loader to hone their skills on shooting, loading, working as a team, and in conjunction with other guns who may be on either or both sides.

The school coaches are available also to take note of any difficulties with specific targets when shooting these flushes. The coach will then go with a particular gun and have a number of such targets thrown to sort out the problem. He is used to this: on most Mondays through the game season his phone will be busy with game shots who ring and book an hour or more, the usual message being, 'I was shooting last week and had a problem with birds coming over high and off left' or whatever. When these people come to the school these awkward targets are thrown and with the aid of the coach the client will soon be taking and breaking them with confidence. Even better, the client should then repeat this success when next shooting live targets. There is no doubt in my opinion that these sportsmen do obtain great pleasure from this regular clay target practice. In addition their live quarry shooting performance improves which increases their pleasure.

*Clay trap. Traps can be lethal: trappers must be briefed, insured, fully protected, and wear ear muffs. Some local bye-laws specify age limits for operators (Essex S.S.)*

*The young entry: Chief coach Ken Davies demonstrating how a coach positions himself to see the shot string and retain control (Holland & Holland S.S.)*

## BUYING ONE'S OWN TRAP FOR PRIVATE PRACTICE

There are an increasing number of clay target and live quarry shooters who do just this. There are pros and cons. A clay trap can be a danger to life and limb if handled improperly. Sadly there has been one fatal accident due to a clay target trap. The prudent will buy a clay trap and have the vendor or maker provide tuition on the safe installation and handling of the trap. All traps must be firmly fixed to prevent them going 'walkabout' when in use. The trapper must be protected from the trap, targets or bits of target, and shot pellets. The shot pellets must drop in a safe area. In addition there are local by-laws which state age limits for the trappers. Before the trap is bought or private clay shooting is attempted it is well worthwhile to become a member of the CPSA, the parent body of the sport (see address at rear of this book). They supply members with splendid advice, including their booklets, on anything to do with the safe shooting of clay targets and other aspects of the sport. This includes insurance.

When first allowing a novice to try clay target shooting one should always use a snap cap in a known-to-be-empty gun. This provides him with the opportunity to become aware of the pressure required to release the trigger. To hand a novice a loaded gun without prior practice with a snap cap usually results in him pulling the trigger prematurely and maybe even firing the gun dangerously. Correctly operated, a private trap installation can be a sound investment. The young entry can be thrown simple going-away targets time after time on exactly the same trajectories.

The use of the snap cap allows the target to be tracked and when the picture is right the trigger will be pulled. This use of the snap cap cuts down the expense, reduces the recoil and allows the young entry to learn how to handle his gun safely. The coach or whoever is standing close behind will carefully note where the barrel muzzle is pointing in relation to the flight of the target.

*Selection of modern clay targets: (from top left to bottom right)* **zz target which has a spinning flight (to score the white centre has to be knocked out); battue target; 3 rabbit targets; mini target; midi or super 90 target; standard target**

Anyone with normal eyesight should soon be able to establish muzzle gun point and clay target relationship, all this while standing close behind a youngster. Any good coach can explain and teach this technique. As the young entry improves his performance he or she will be allowed to use a few live cartridges. Over shooting, i.e., firing large numbers of cartridges by the young or indeed almost anyone can be a mistake. Each shot must be analysed, and the appropriate remedy applied where necessary. It is well worthwhile always to watch carefully how any clay target is being broken. If for instance only the left-hand side of a target is being broken this means that the pattern is being placed slightly off to the left of the target. If targets are being consistently broken only on the bottom skirt, this is an indication that the shot pattern is low each time. The muzzle point must be raised slightly to centre the pattern on the following targets.

No trap should ever be left cocked and unattended. No unauthorized person should be allowed to operate any trap. Improperly used traps can be dangerous; it is up to the owner to obtain advice *before use*. Adequate protection for the eyes, ears, and anatomy of coach, trapper, and pupil is essential. The fallout area for shot, clay target and bits of target should be kept free of humans and any other living things at all times.

# 22

# Safety and More Efficient Gun Handling

## THE *CPSA* CONTRIBUTION

In the early days long-established clay clubs seemed to have one or more of their wise elders readily available and willing to offer quiet kindly words of advice on safe competent gun handling. These elders had the experience plus the expertise to iron out any problems arising. This ability was useful to help new members to become safe shots and accepted members of the club. The tyro cannot be expected to realize at first just how lethal a shotgun can be if carelessly or foolishly handled. Those who were coming into the sport previously never having even seen a shotgun could not be expected to know how to conform safely. The rough shooter who previously had operated as a loner had only himself to worry about. At clay clubs there are usually a considerable number of members moving about and carrying shotguns. So a form of shooting etiquette or safe behaviour based on good manners and common sense became established and was religiously observed at the best clubs.

When clay shooting booms, as it does every decade or so, there will be groups of people who wish to take up clay shooting at club level and yet do not, indeed cannot be expected to, realize the pitfalls of running a clay club. Even worse there is no hard core of older experienced members to provide guidance as at the older established clubs. Although the club secretary and committee of the new clubs may wish to help their members they may be too busy with the day-to-day running of the club to cope with showing new members the ropes as far as safe shooting is concerned. The CPSA membership has grown from hundreds to over twenty thousand in the past thirty years, and is still growing. The CPSA executive is well aware of the problems of new clubs and club members. Years ago the executive read the writing on the wall and, to promote safer shooting for their members, instigated the CPSA club coaches award scheme. The writer was co-opted on to the CPSA coaching committee as long ago as 1973. Since that time the CPSA has actively encouraged the appointment of a CPSA club safety officer and a CPSA club coach at every affiliated club. The coaching committee organized courses for club safety officers, referees and coaches. The writer was the first National Coach and Safety Officer. The 'Ten Commandments for Safe Shooting' produced, most affiliated clay clubs now have a safety officer. The CPSA executive rightly advocates that every member must always act as his own safety officer. It is their 'finger on the trigger' when they are clay shooting at any club. The majority of members have always been extremely careful, willingly acting as examples to new members, providing a back-up to the club safety officers. There is an officially appointed safety officer at most affiliated clubs.

The CPSA will supply newly affiliated clubs with booklets explaining how to start a clay club and how to programme its safe day-to-day organization; all this for a low affiliation fee and the price of an s.a.e. All members of affiliated clubs should in their own interests be paid-up members of the CPSA. As such they are automatically insured for third-party claims for a million pounds.

## The CPSA Coaches Award Scheme

Instigated by the executive 17 years ago, it has proved to be a great success. Now the CPSA has held some 23 of these coaches' courses. As a result there are hundreds of club coaches operating at affiliated clubs in all parts of the country. These coaches are a great help, especially for beginner members, ensuring they handle their guns with increasing proficiency and behave safely at all times.

Coaching courses have also been successfully held in Scotland in conjunction with the SCPSA. At the present, due to the success of previous courses there is a long waiting list of applicants who wish to become CPSA coaches. Therefore the CPSA have planned three courses for this year to shorten the waiting period. It is encouraging that some CPSA coaches have progressed and are now running their own successful shooting schools. A notable example is ex-development officer Mike Alldis at his Essex shooting school.

The activities of both CPSA coaches and those who have gone commercial has helped the continuing growth of CPSA clubs and facilities, with rising standards of safe gun handling and shooting at all levels, new members being made welcome by the safety officers and encouraged by club coaches to handle and shoot their guns safely and competently.

## Why Become a Club Coach?

There are many reasons: some members are good shots who have so enjoyed their shooting they wish to put something back and help others obtain enjoyment; these people usually make good coaches and their enthusiasm is an asset to any club.

Others hope that by coaching others their own performance may improve. By constantly watching the clay target trajectories as thrown for clients it is true that most coaches become more adept at reading target line and trajectory. This may or may not improve a coach's shooting performance. The late Jack Wright – the father of isu Skeet in this country – once told me 'it is all too easy for a coach to acquire all the faults perpetrated by his clients'. Most coaches, myself included, find this very true after coaching a beginner on slow easy dolly birds and then attempting to shoot high speed targets oneself. Others just like being involved in anything to do with clay shooting.

## How to Become a Club Coach

First become a paid up member of the cpsa. Then with the help of the club safety officer and the club coach learn the rudiments of safe gun handling. As soon as these two officials think it is advisable our 'would-be coach' should apply to attend a course of instruction and eventually obtain the cpsa 'Certificate of Competence'. This certificate will state the applicant 'has satisfied the Board of Examiners after a course of instruction, that he or she is considered competent in the use and handling of a shotgun for clay pigeon shooting'. The instructions given on the course are clear and concise. Advice is given on safe gun handling, firing point behaviour, etc. Eventually it is hoped most cpsa members will successfully take this course.

## Practical Work on Certificate of Competence Course

At first as always, until the member has proved to be a safe gun operator, all gun handling will be done with the aid of snap caps. These are in effect dummy cartridges. By the use of these snap caps, even if a mistake is made, the trigger pulled by accident and the gun action goes click, no harm will have been done. The mistake will be thoroughly analysed and remedial action taken. Contrast this with the old method of beginning with live rounds; there a mistake could be lethal at the worst, frightening at best. Then there is a short thirty-minute theory paper, designed to require a minimum of writing, with true/false boxes to tick. When the course organizers are satisfied on all aspects of safety there will be a final session during which live ammunition will be shot. Thereby demonstrating the safe usage of guns at all times by the member taking the certificate course.

After obtaining his certificate the would-be club coach should hone his own shooting performance. The ability to produce a top performance does help any coach's credibility as far as his future pupils are concerned. At least six months before attending a coaching course the candidate should approach his club coach and ask if it is possible to attend his coaching sessions. In the early days of the scheme it was difficult to find a club coach as they were spread very thinly around. Now that most clubs have a resident coach this makes life easier. It must be realized there can be no substitute for 'doing'. Most club coaches will be delighted to have a would-be coach as an unpaid assistant. For instance when coaching targets are being released on the button, to have a helper operate this button allows the club coach to have both hands free and be able to exercise more control over his pupil.

The trainee will be shown how to test for master eye, to check gun fit and mount, to set up the pupil to the easier targets, and to help a client adapt himself to an ill-fitting gun. He will be expected to explain the principles of breaking targets safely while using the CPSA method. The CPSA 'method' for breaking clay targets although not new was evolved by Clarrie Wilson as a result of a time and motion study. Basically it consists of accurately pointing the gun muzzles at moving targets, then with gun and shooter locked together as one unit, moving the muzzles out in front and on the target line. Once the muzzles are far enough out in front of the target the trigger is pulled without check of swing. All this plus fault diagnosis and correction and safe pupil handling will be practised until it becomes second nature. Until the candidate can explain the principles and teach the method to a novice while shooting safely a coaching certificate will not be awarded.

## Gun Know-How

It is always worthwhile to ask one's regular gun shop for help in recognizing the various proof marks and assessing whether a gun, as it should be, is in proof and in a sound shootable condition. Gun shop staff are busy so do *not* go into the gun shop on a busy Saturday afternoon, when the shop is full of customers. Make an appointment and attend at a time mutually convenient. Guns with loose-off-the-face actions, dents, bulges, excessive barrel pitting, loose ribs, too light trigger pulls, triggers 'hard on' and safety catches which jar back or slip off, can be hazards to all and sundry within 300 yards. The club coach should for his or her own protection have some knowledge of these problems. The ammunition being shot should be suitable for the gun in use.

## Taking the Coaching Award Course

The would-be coach will again be shown how to explain and teach the 'method'. Due to his previous work with his own club coach he should be able to do just this to any beginner given to him while on the coaching course. He should soon realize that this method is a fine ploy to teach the beginner how to shoot most moving targets.

## Master Eye

He will be shown a simple method to test for eye dominance. Due to pre-course work he should be easily able to do this test: Take the known empty and closed gun, have the pupil fold his arms, place the gun butt in the shoulder pocket. The coach will stand 6 feet in front of the client and have him point the gun at the coach's right eye with both eyes open and check which eye is master.

## Gun Fitting

The course takes place over a weekend, in which time it is impossible to provide the candidates with little more than the rudiments. It is unrealistic to expect a would-be club coach to become an expert gun fitter in one short weekend. This knowledge takes years to acquire, yet the would-be coach should know if the gun being used is a reasonable fit. If not he should be able to help his pupil fit himself to his gun until such time that he can go to a shooting school and obtain an expert fitting.

A good club coach should be able to diagnose gun handling faults. By standing close behind the pupil/guinea pig and looking closely and directly over his shoulder one can observe barrel–target relationship and subsequent pattern placement. Also one can prescribe the remedy which will turn missing into hitting. Seeing shot string is not always easy as much depends on the conditions of light. But with practice on barrel–target relationship one can usually be fairly sure where a target is being missed regardless whether the shot is seen in flight or not.

The best target for coaching the beginner is the slightly rising straight away. With a pre-mounted trap stocked gun which throws its pattern slightly high all the client has to do is to point at the target and more or less shoot straight at it as it appears to be sitting on the front sight of the muzzles. To teach the shooting of incomers to a novice can be very dangerous. All incoming targets, when broken, tend to shower the shooter and anyone near him with target fragments. For this reason all should wear safety glasses and head and body protection.

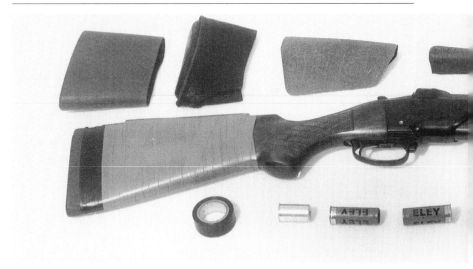

*Brno skeet gun weight 7 lb. with muzzle brakes, Sorbothane pad on comb. Parker-Hale Pachmayre decelerator recoil pad with short toe. Bottom row **tape, snap cap, Eley light load trainer cartridges, Scott .410 adaptor, trigger pull tester, safety glasses.** Top row **stock boots, comb raisers***

*Some of the equipment used by a club coach. Left to right top **trigger tester, three types of ear muffs, Peltor, Parker-Hale and Peltor, tape, snap cap,** bottom left **rubber stock boot, Nickerson Sorbothane stock boot, safety goggles, comb raisers, hand guard, obliterator, M. Allen 'Stock Fitta'***

## Ear Protection

Whether one is coaching or being taught, hearing protection is a must. Go to any shoot and listen to the shooters standing about in the entries tent: one will hear 'what, *what* did you say'. This is the result of much

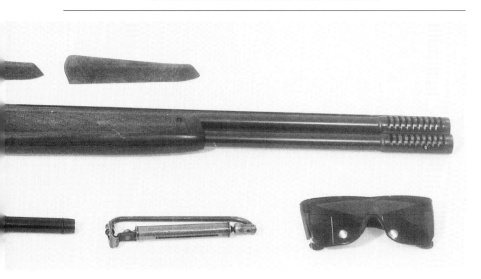

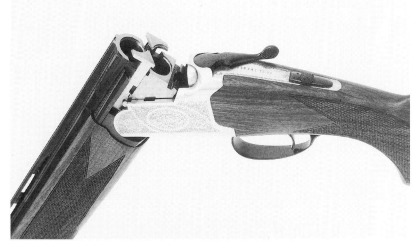

***Lanber o/u Sporter with screw-in choke tubes, as used by the Shooting
Box for coaching and company days***

shooting with no ear protection. Be warned. The general opinion is that
ear muffs are better than ear plugs. Always obtain the latest and most up-
to-date advice from the club safety officer.

Snap caps are an essential part of the coach's equipment. The novice
must be taught the exact pressure required to release the trigger. This
can be done with snap caps, there being an absence of recoil and muzzle
blast all of which assists the client to 'call his shots'.

The club practice trap should be well isolated from the rest of the club
shooting stands. As all coaches know well, to allow other shooters who
have had even a small amount of experience to shoot in the same squad as

genuine beginners is traumatic. Within minutes all the squad are coaching, all giving different answers, the result being the real beginner does not know who to believe and ends up disheartened and believing no-one, not even the coach.

## Club Guns

The larger clubs have a gun for coaching new members. For mature members this gun should be of full weight, open bored, with fairly high comb, soft recoil pad and a short-toed stock. A small gauge gun can be an advantage when in use by the young ladies amongst the younger entry.

## The Ammunition for Coaching

*Usual* shooting school practice is to use as light a shot load as possible and as heavy a gun. Eley produce a 12 bore Trainer cartridge with a $\frac{7}{8}$ oz. load. Other makers produce similar 12 bore cartridges with a load of 1 oz. or less size 7 shot which is ample. Game gun owners will also find these light loads ideal for practice clays. The coach must be in complete charge and not allow overshooting; if a novice does this and gets hurt he will not return. Any chancy or risky gun handling must be checked at once. One mistake is one too many. Some clients bring small children and marauding dogs; these are distractions and should be forbidden. Shooting must be regarded as a sport of responsibility.

# 23

# The Shooting
# School Coach

## THE ROLE OF THE COACH

THESE people are the elite among shooting coaches. What is a coach, and what does he do or attempt to do? Many of those who do shoot muddle the duties and qualities of a coach with those of a shooting instructor.

The shooting instructor is one who instructs; he will instruct the pupil until that pupil can mechanically perform safe gun handling and its efficient shooting almost by rote or numbers to the limits of his desire and/or competence at that time. It is unusual for any instructor to delve too deeply into the psychological aspects of any pastime he is teaching. The true coach will be able to explain correct shooting technique if given the opportunity, a willing pupil and the amount of time required for this purpose. The coach will take the pupil through a complete and progressive course of planned action, rather than allow the indiscriminate firing of cartridges with little explanation of how and why. The successful coach has been trained and can do this time after time. If not, he would not remain a coach for very long.

### Ambitions of the Client

Any success achieved will depend on the pupil, his approach and co-operation. There are many people who just wish to shoot. Once they have acquired the knowledge of how to break simple targets successfully they 'stick'. Although many of these 'stickers' realize that to the inexpert onlooker this successful and repetitive breaking of targets does in fact look much harder than it actually is, they are perfectly content to roll up at a shooting school and spend an hour on maybe five different stands shooting easy targets. They will usually shoot 20 cartridges on each stand. The targets will be thrown and flying on fixed simple trajectories.

The client will know exactly when and where each target will appear; he will, by constant practice, kill most of these targets easily. But he will not wish to shoot at any target which varies even a foot from its expected trajectory. The reason for this being that he has progressed as far as he can be bothered to or wishes. An experienced coach knows this well; he is also aware when clients with this attitude of mind have reached their ceiling. Clients with this outlook rarely progress beyond becoming a mediocre shot. When such clients have become as competent as they wish the coach should tell them so. They are in effect wasting the time and cost of a top-class coach. They would be equally well served hiring an instructor who can arrange the throwing of such simple targets and explain where any of these targets are missed.

There will be other clients who wish to concentrate on one particular facet or discipline of shooting. This may be a specialized form of live quarry shooting such as the high-driven pheasant. Even then clients will vary in their attitudes. Some will wish to shoot the straight incomer at all times; they will learn how to cope with this target and when they subsequently go about their high-driven pheasants days will only take the straight birds which they know they can hit fairly consistently, leaving any slightly angling incomers to neighbouring guns. These people will often be regarded as excellent performers and possess a good average on the birds they take. This average is often much higher than that put up by the better shots who happily shoot at and take any birds which can be called their legitimate birds and which are in range. These last clients are a joy to coach. When on a visit to the school they will warm up on a few straight incomers, and then actually ask the coach to call 'vary them'. The trapper will joyfully vary the driven targets on either side of the incomer. This is done by placing the targets on the trap arm or by swinging the trap about. Either way the targets will be less easy to kill but the shooter will find this variation of the high-driven target a great help in improving footwork and understanding the 'best place to take such targets'.

There is little unanimity among people on how they stand to take high-driven varied targets. The young agile person can point his front foot nearly straight forward on a direct line towards the trap and tower, and while leaving his feet in this position, take his birds as incomers or as high crossers depending on the targets and the angles thrown. The elderly and/or the arthritic usually find they can take these targets more easily with less stress and bodily strain if they move their feet as soon as they see and read the targets. They will be moving their feet to the most suitable position as soon as the target comes in view. For instance the first target may be a real screamer coming wide of the shooter's left shoulder. To contact with this target the gun will have to be pushed well up and well forward. Those with young bodies can easily perform this while shooting off their centrally pointed front foot. Older people with stiffening muscles prefer to move their feet and take that target as a high crosser.

Other clients will wish to study and discuss the theory of shooting and guns in depth. Others will spend hours patterning their guns with almost every known combination of cartridge and shot size, often getting so bogged down in the theory, that this knowledge has an adverse effect on their practical performance. So much so that if they see even a small hole in one of their test patterns on the plate their confidence in whatever the combination of choke, pellet size and shot load used will be destroyed. When dealing with such clients the coach has to persuade, cajole, or even order his client to alter his ways. When a client's performance deteriorates, the coach provides a shoulder for that client to cry on. His wide experience allows him to ascertain while watching his client shoot and, by talking guns and shooting, whether the reason for the decline in performance is physical, mental, or as so often happens, a combination of both.

Some clients will be highly strung; others may be of a more placid temperament. The coach will treat every client as a separate entity as befits his mental approach and physical behaviour. Shooters, being human, are complex creatures: full of every imaginable phobia, which will either develop confidence or inhibitions in the client if given the slightest opportunity. It is up to the coach to dig out the real problem and then provide the reasoned remedy.

The good coach will carefully keep written records of his assessment of clients on both their mental and physical capabilities. He will also keep details of any gun(s) used. All of which can have a bearing on future performance. Eventually the coach will be able to guesstimate what the problem is likely to be before the client even loads his gun.

## Other Coaching Aids

There is no doubt that the modern video camera and screen – if correctly used – can prove a great asset to the coach. Before the advent of the video camera some coaches made full use of the Polaroid instant camera. This allowed the coach to back up his arguments with actual pictures showing the client in action. The whole gamut of sloppy gun mounting, head movement, poor stance, barrel–target relationship, in fact the full sequence of the faults perpetrated up to the time when the target was missed are visible. All these faults were shown in still photography but

*The traditional textbook method of closing a gun by lifting up the toe of the gun stock is often too difficult for the young shot. If the gun is new and stiff, or otherwise hard to close, the wrists of the young are not strong enough to close the gun and still control the muzzles*

now the video can show this in normal or slow motion. Some American schools have video cameras providing instant playback and diagnosis.

In the early days of the CPSA coaches award scheme the video camera was used on the courses; in those days the batteries were of limited capacity. Even so it was then proved that there was a bright future for the video when used by an expert operator both for pinpointing mistakes and providing better and more easily understood and applied coaching precepts. The client can help his coach in many ways: it is a waste of good money and unfair treatment of a coach for any client to rush through his work, leave his business at the last minute, drive many miles at high speed, then expect at the end of all this rushing about to be completely relaxed and in a calm and receptive frame of mind for coaching.

Competent shooting requires good visual acuity, split-second timing, steady nerves and reflexes, plus complete and 100 per cent concentration on the job in hand by coach, shooter and trapper.

Some clients will bring their partially trained dog – 'to get him used to the gun fire and attain experience'. To attempt to coach such people while they are ejaculating 'Sit Toby *sit*', or while they are fiddling with a silent dog whistle or whatever, is a complete waste of everyone's time and money: the only result being the production of a fine crop of ulcers for the coach. Not even the dog will derive any benefit, although it may have been lucky to escape being shot by 'accident' or design.

Small children, friends and other perambulating landmarks are an added distraction for both coach and client and best left at home. Exceptions are understanding uncles, aunts, parents and friends. If they really understand and are prepared to remain unobtrusive in the background they will obtain a great deal of pleasure not only from paying for the lessons but as observers watching how their offspring develop, growing in confidence and stature in the able hands of an understanding coach. An added benefit is if the person paying for the lessons is a shooting person who has never had a shooting lesson – then he too will learn much. He will see for himself how the coach teaches the young entry to open, load, and close a gun, while all the time being very well aware of his gun point. The old classical method of opening and closing a gun is I believe outmoded and very difficult, if not impossible, for any youngster to perform safely.

The old books showed the owner closing the gun by means of placing one hand on the stock toe and lifting up the stock, rather than lifting up the barrels and allowing the muzzles to be held about at waist level. This is fine if the owner is big and beefy; also if the gun is easy to open and close. Some guns, especially when new, are very tightly jointed and a normal youngster has not the strength in his wrists to open or close a gun in such a manner. If he does try, what will happen is shown in the sequence of photos. The muzzles will be dipped due to the leverage of the stock and action against the boy's weak wrist which is trying to hold the

*The Churchill method. The stock is rested on the hip and trapped there by pressure of the forearm resulting in a solid lockup of stock and shooter. This provides superior leverage and positive gun control*

*After the top lever has been fully pushed across, the front hand pulls the barrels down and around in a low arc to the left with muzzles pointing safely towards the ground at all times*

*With the gun fully open a pair of empty cartridge cases are loaded for the purpose of this demonstration*

*Again with the stock trapped between forearm and hip the gun is closed by moving the front hand and barrels around in a safe low right arc*

*To open the gun after the triggers have been pulled, the stock is kept trapped against the hip and the top lever pushed fully over. The front hand once more pulls the barrels around and across in the same safe low arc*

*This gun position ensures on opening that the empties are thrown well clear of the shooter's face and body and across to his rear right. Observe how on this particular gun – Miroku – the ejectors are correctly timed with both empty cases ejected at the same time and closely together*

muzzles pointing safely at all times. Moreover it is rare that one sees anyone in a hot drive take his hand from the stock wrist and place it on the stock toe. The alternative method in the photos was demonstrated to me half a century ago by Robert Churchill and still works today.

The young entry will first be taught the above plus the rest of basic safe gun handling. Very briefly this entails first checking that any gun he picks up is unloaded. Then he is taught to safely load and unload, always keeping his gun pointing safely. Once he has begun to hit targets and had a session at the pattern plate, subject to the coach's approval, it will be great fun for both the young one and the provider of the cash to shoot.

The coach will provide testing targets to suit the capabilities of both clients, giving young and old a common ground for subsequent discussion. Again, with the coach's connivance, the great majority of clients can if they so wish be taught by the coach just how and where to stand behind a friend or young entry to ascertain where a target is being missed. I know many youngsters who have been shown how to do this. When a parent and young person are sharing a day's shooting, each can help the other with their shooting. Further lessons are always a good idea; constant practice is fine. When difficulties arise on shooting for real the coach is always ready and very able at the school to iron out any problems. Being a properly trained observer he sees most of the game.

## The loader

Any sportsman who tries to shoot with a pair of guns and an untrained loader is chancing his arm, very often even his life and the lives of others. The safe loading and reloading of the shotgun when birds are streaming over and safely exchanging that loaded shotgun with the empty or at times half-empty gun from the owner has always required concentrated and constant practice. Victorian sportsmen spent hours with their loader for weeks before the season commenced. It was alleged that one old-time sportsman was found late at night in his host's library practising gun handling and gun exchange with his personal loader.

In these modern times loading practice and training can be done at a good shooting school under the watchful eye of the resident coach, each of whom has his own methods. It is usual to begin with a handful of snap caps and clays thrown over at random with the gun and his loader working on their drill. It is up to each team to decide after consultation with the coach what the attitude to safety catches shall be and firmly stick to it. There may be safety catch problems these days with some American visitors. Their guns often have non-automatic safety catches which stay put unless moved manually. The usual 'best' British gun will automatically return its safety catch to the 'safe' position each time the gun is opened. Even in the great days around the turn of the century when shooting double guns with a loader was common, each shooter was a law

*A good coach makes shooting lessons safe and great fun* (K. Davies, Holland & Holland S.S.)

unto himself. One famous Victorian who shot with a pair of hammer guns which had to be manually cocked always insisted that the loader cocked both hammers after loading and before returning that gun to the shooter. A modern sportsman when confronted with a loader of unknown quality must decide whether it is more prudent to use only the one gun. Then he can fire, open his one gun as and when he decides, holding it in such a manner as to allow his loader to drop in the cartridge(s) as required. It is surprising how quickly a single gun can be handled in this manner. But the barrels of this one gun so shot will rapidly become very hot; a good hand guard on the barrels plus a glove on the shooter's front hand will help. The prudent sportsman will allow enough time before the game season begins to have his coach teach both loader and himself the correct drill on how to either safely handle and shoot a pair of guns, or shoot a single gun with assistance to load and reload that one gun.

# 24

# Sportsman's Time and Swing

## PROBLEMS OF PLACING THE PELLET PATTERN ON THE TARGET

THESE are many: as far as the theory is concerned some factors are constant. For instance if a well-known make of cartridge is always used, the manufacturers of that cartridge can supply the velocity of the shot. This would seem to be a comparatively simple exercise. And yet the first fact to be established is how and where the pellet velocities are taken.

### Velocities

Years ago it was standard practice to give cartridge velocities as 'observed velocities'. These figures are established by taking the pellet speed over the first 20 yds. Other cartridge makers chronograph the velocity of the pellets as they leave the muzzle. This is 'muzzle velocity' and obviously if the same batch of cartridges are tested for both 'muzzle' and 'observed velocity' the 'muzzle velocity' will be higher than the 'observed velocity'. Many years ago legend had it that one cartridge maker sold his own brand of 'high velocity' cartridges. Certainly the figures given were higher than that attained by most cartridges as then advertised. It was found that in fact the figures given were actually 'muzzle velocity' and that the 'observed velocity' over the 20 yards was in fact similar to that of most standard cartridges available at that time and in reality not high velocity at all.

Observed velocity over the 20 yds is also greatly influenced by the size of the shot. For instance the following examples are taken from Burrard, *The Modern Shotgun*, Volume 2: The Cartridge, 1985.

| Observed Velocity 1000 F.S | Muzzle Velocity | 20 yds | 30 yds |
|---|---|---|---|
| Shot size 6 | 1,162 | 835 | 709 |
| Shot size 9 | 1,242 | 796 | 640 |

Note the higher muzzle velocity of size 9 shot and its lower velocity at 30 yds compared with size 6 shot. Tests which I have done when shooting various shot sizes at pattern plates at 40 yds plus have also established just how quickly small shot of size 9 may drift sideways. Also the lowering trajectory of small shot when fired against strong head winds will cause the point of impact compared with the point of aim to say 50 yds to be much lower. This factor is rarely appreciated by shooters who are prone to 'stretch their barrels' and attempt longish shots. In fact to attempt long range shots when shooting such small shot as 9 does inevitably mean that, instead of the target being centred in the pellet pattern of a killing circle of maybe 40 in diameter, due to the pattern placement being low, the shooter is in fact trying to hit the target with a tiny segment of the centre top of the pattern which may in effect be only 1 in by maybe 3 in. A vast difference.

## Sportsman's Time

There are three vital periods which added together make up the total time from the sportsman's mind willing the trigger pull to the time when the shot actually impinges or otherwise on the target. These are:

1 'Sportsman's time', i.e., the time from the mind willing the finger to the time when that trigger is actually pulled. This is and always has been a variable between different sportsmen. Any coach is aware that human reflexes vary greatly even with one particular individual from minute to minute and day to day. Some seem to have almost instantaneous reflexes; others seem to dither, taking seemingly aeons of time. Strangely enough this dithering if consistent may help the shooter, especially if he is one who shoots without pause as he swings through the target. This dithering does allow the muzzles to be swung further out in front of the target due to the longer time taken.

2 'Time up the barrel': this is the time lapse from when the trigger is actually pulled until the cartridge has been fired and the shot has travelled to the gun muzzles. This is usually measured from the actual hammer fall.

3 'Time of flight': this is the total time from the pellets leaving the

muzzles up to when they make contact on a target normally 25 to 35 yards away. This time can and will vary, being influenced by many factors: the speed of the shot charge and the size of the shot being the most important.

Burrard calculated as did others that a bird or target travelling at 40 m.p.h will cover one yard in $\frac{1}{20}$ second, and of course 20 yards in one second, for most people one second of time is roughly taken by them speaking the words 'one thousand'. He also calculated a charge of shot will take $\frac{1}{20}$ second to travel 20 yards, $\frac{1}{10}$ second to travel 30 yards, and $\frac{1}{7}$ second to travel 40 yards. If this is so, it is essential for the muzzles to be pointing out ahead of the target for target and shot to collide. This is termed 'lead' and is approximately one yard for 20 yds, and two yards for 30 yds.

The Eley Shooters Diary shows the above times in a slightly different guise but the end result is similar. For consistent performance there must be consistent timing; this will reduce the variables to allow one to build up a regular sight picture for most targets. What should then happen is that the target is seen, its flight and speed almost automatically estimated and the muzzles placed on the target or its line of flight or wherever is one's normal technique. This sets off a natural reaction of swing and shoot.

## Swing

It is generally agreed among sportsmen and women that moving targets are best and most consistently shot by means of a moving gun. Myself and many others have experimented and established that it is indeed possible to intercept targets and break them successfully. The technique for this interception is to select a spot in the sky at a sufficient distance in front of the moving target and pull the trigger while the gun is in fact stationary. The majority find this a harder technique to acquire than locking up a mounted gun into the shoulder pocket, with man and gun swinging along the target line in similar fashion to that of a gun and its turret. Most find the 'swing through' system more effective than the stationary 'spot in the sky' technique.

## Speed of Swing

Game shooters at the beginning of the game season will often visit a shooting school for a refresher course. Often on the first visit the sportsman will be told he is shooting behind his targets. The experienced coach will know exactly whether his client is a 'swing through', 'come from behind' or 'gap shooter'.

This problem of placing the shot pattern further in front is then tackled differently depending on the client's technique. It is normal for the

*A well-loved gun is but a well-loved tool.*
*Percy Stanbury with his W.&C. Scott s/s gun. For most of his shooting*
*life of over 50 years 'Stan' used this gun for everything, winning almost*
*all there was to be won in the clay shooting world. The fact that it was*
*bored full seemed not to worry him at all. He won Sporting, Skeet and*
*Down the Line championships with it. He also used it for all his live*
*quarry shooting. A prime example of the one-gun man*

swing-through shooter to believe that he is indeed using the same technique as he used last season. So he may, the only difference being that his speed of swing is now slightly slower due to his technique being rusty. In this case the coach will suggest that the client increases the speed of swing-through. This increase will result in the muzzles being pushed further out in front of the target and success will be achieved. As for the 'gap shooter', if he is missing the coach will suggest the client opens up the gap he is seeing; success should follow. The problem is that it is early in the season and the client is not yet shooting with his mid-season aggressiveness. In fact he is not 'shooting savage'.

## Effect of swing

There are many who believe that the swing of the gun muzzles will impart the same amount of swing to the shot column and that the flight of the charge is similar to that imparted to a jet of water from a hose pipe. This is not so. The shot column may only be an inch in length as it leaves the muzzles. The time taken for the departure of the front end of the shot column and its tail end from the gun muzzles has been estimated as less than one ten thousandth part of a second, during which time one's gun barrels will have hardly changed their direction at all. Therefore the water jet effect as in the hose pipe cannot be simulated.

The result of checking one's swing is very different. If one agrees with the time taken for the shot to travel from muzzles to a 30 yd target, which has been estimated as $\frac{1}{10}$ of a second. The target will travel some six feet in that time. Therefore to check the swing will result in that target being missed by a couple of yards, quite a distance.

## Importance of Velocity

Eley tables show that the difference between high velocity and normal velocity cartridges means only a distance of four inches extra lead being required when taking targets at a 30 yd range. This may seem small, yet the best shots watch how their targets are being broken or their quarry is being killed. If the trailing edge of the target is being hit with the leading edge of the shot string, or if birds are being tailored, that shooter will place his shot string and patterns further forward when taking subsequent targets or live quarry. This he will achieve either by swinging his gun faster or opening up his sight picture. Although one is writing about milliseconds of time, the expert can cope; that is why he is an expert shot. Any sportsman or woman can with practice become used to cartridges of almost any velocity. Over many years experience has shown without a doubt that the most consistent results will be achieved by the person who learns to shoot with one particular brand of cartridge and one well-fitted gun. With practice he will know well and have confidence in the performance of gun, cartridge and his own capabilities. All other combinations of gun and cartridge will be eschewed. In time that gun will seem to have acquired a balance as fine as the scales of justice and will be handled in similar fashion as a craftsman handles one of his well-loved tools or as a violinist plays his violin. All will work together in harmony to produce a fine performance. To hanker after strange gods in the shape of different velocity cartridges or guns only results in producing more variables and increasingly inconsistent performances.

## Shotgun Marksmanship Basics

There are three established methods to obtain lead – forward allowance – to compensate for sportsman's time, time up the barrels, time of flight.

1 'Swing through smoke trail'. Start with muzzles behind target and on target line, overtake, firing as one swings through and ahead of the target.

2 'CPSA method'. Place muzzles on target, keeping on target line swing muzzles in front of target to obtain lead and fire.

3 'Maintain lead'. Place muzzles ahead on estimated line of target, when the gap between muzzles and target seems correct fire.

All these methods work, much depends on the visual acuity and co-ordination of the shooter, experienced shots have evolved their own method, they may use any of the above depending on speed, distance, and type of target. Whatever method of obtaining lead to compensate for sportsman's time is used, unless the muzzles are the proper distance in front of targets requiring forward allowance, the target will be missed – usually behind.

# 25
## Cartridges

## TESTING AND COMPARING SHOT VELOCITIES AND PENETRATION

IT has long been established that it is possible to test shotgun cartridges for the velocity of the shot charge and compare the performance of one brand with another. This can be accomplished by means of easily knocked up equipment by any layman. He will certainly not require the aid of an expensive chronograph.

Years ago one could buy Pettits pads. Each pad consisted of 45 sheets of $9\frac{1}{2} \times 10\frac{1}{2}$ in paper. These pads were fastened together at the corners but it was a simple enough matter to separate them to see how many sheets the pellets of the shot charge had penetrated. Payne-Gallwey and many other old-time investigators used them, although most claimed that these sheets of paper varied in thickness and toughness. Payne-Gallwey therefore preferred to separate the sheets and designed a special open-ended copper tube type rack with slits sawn down it at intervals of $\frac{3}{4}$ in. By inserting a sheet of paper in each slot, then standing at a known yardage from the end of the copper tube it was possible to shoot directly at the end of the tube and ascertain just how many sheets of Pettits paper were then penetrated by the shot pellets. Some twenty years ago the author worked in collaboration with Gough Thomas in a series of experiments on chamberless shotguns. This was to compare the velocity and penetration from chambered and chamberless guns.

We made up a rack or trough from three pieces of wood. The bottom

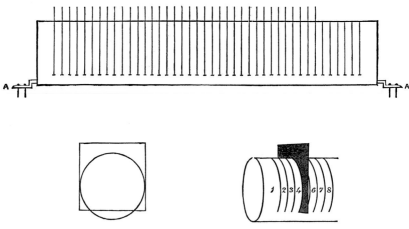

**Payne-Gallwey's rack**

plank was 8 in wide, 30 in long, and $\frac{5}{8}$ in thick. Each of the sides were $8 \times 30 \times \frac{5}{8}$ in thick. Sawcuts $\frac{1}{8}$ in deep and 1 in apart were made across the three pieces of wood. These pieces of wood were screwed together in the form of a trough with the sawcuts coinciding along the inside and bottom of the trough. Instead of the Pettits pads which are now unobtainable we used what is known in the stationery trade as 10 sheet-thick card. This card is available in large sheets, each sheet when cut produces some 12 portions of card measuring $7\frac{1}{2}$ in square. The approximate card thickness was $\frac{1}{40}$ in. Each saw cut was numbered beginning with 1 at the end of the trough which was pointed towards the shooter. The cards in the rack were also numbered in the same sequence. This numbering is helpful as it allows one to look down into the rack of cards and see just how many cards are penetrated by the pellets from whatever cartridge is being tested. After a single cartridge has been fired at the end of the trough/ card rack, each card from number one is taken out in turn, each shot hole where the pellet has penetrated through a card is recorded, the shot hole ringed and the card returned into its saw cuts. The pellets in the bottom of the trough between the cards are counted and removed. When fully documented, another cartridge can be shot at the cards in the trough and tested in the same manner. The cards can be used more than once depending on the number of shot holes they acquire. Dents in the cards are disregarded.

The distance at which the gun stands from the card trough end must be carefully measured, not guessed otherwise errors are inevitable. We chose 30 yards as the best distance from which to shoot, this being the top range at which most sportsmen take their game. We wore safety glasses as a precaution against ricochets. Those who normally take their game at closer or longer ranges can shoot at card racks from the distance they prefer. The cards must be stored in dry conditions as dampness will cause variations in penetration between cartridges on test.

Brister in his book *Shotgunning* made up and used a similar gadget for his experiments. As a back-up to these experiments he enlisted the help of his wife and a station-wagon and trailer which had a long sheet of paper fixed to the side to study shot stringing. In the shot stringing experiments he proved that soft shot even if of the same size and pellet weight did produce a longer shot string due to the greater pellet deformation which occurred with the softer shot.

It is essential to equate like with like. One cannot take one batch of cartridges loaded with size 6 shot and another loaded with size 4 shot. (See the tables in the preceding chapter showing the effect of shot sizes on velocity over different distances.) The variation in the weight of the shot will affect the penetration of the shot on the sheets of card.

An equally important factor is the hardness of the shot used. I have found that really hard shot has better penetration than soft shot even when the shot on test is of exactly the same size and weight. The hard shot will provide greater penetration. When a cartridge is fired the force of the explosion and the pressures produced to start and keep pushing a shot charge up and out at the muzzle will cause pellet deformation. The pellets at the bottom of the shot column will be especially affected and pressurized out of round. Obviously the softer the shot the greater the deformation. The passage of the shot charge up the barrel and the shape of the chamber cones and chokes, if any, also have a bearing on this. So of course does the wadding: plastic cup wads do protect the shot charge from abrasion on its path up the barrel. Some original work on shot deformation is in Kynoch's booklet *Shooting Notes and Comments*, 1910.The conclusions obtained from these Kynoch experiments also prove that the larger the shot the greater the maintained velocity at the longer ranges.

Comparing the performance of soft and chilled (hard) shot when fired through cylinder and choke barrels, the combination of choke barrels and soft shot will produce a lower striking velocity at 30 yds than when shot of a similar hardness is fired through a cylinder barrel at the same distance.

The striking velocities of shot at longer ranges than 30 yards was found to depend very largely on the shot retaining its spherical shape, and this retention of shape was helped by a combination of chilled shot and cylinder bored barrels. Half a century after Kynoch's work, Brister's experiments came to the same conclusions.

## Other Factors Affecting Velocity

Poor storage of cartridges has been proved to have a great bearing on shot velocity. Cartridges stored in conditions of extreme cold will show lower than normal velocities when compared with other correctly stored cartridges from the same batch. In similar fashion cartridges taken from a batch and stored in extreme conditions of heat will produce higher velocities than those stored normally.

Cartridge manufacturers have long advised that shotgun cartridges should be carefully stored at normal room temperature. These days, however, with modern houses being almost universally centrally heated, it has been established that many sportsmen now store their cartridges in rooms where the temperature, although normal for these days, is too high for cartridges. Although this is understandable, it is thoughtless and unfair to cartridge makers. It can also be the cause of the high pressures produced when such cartridges are fired. These pressures may be dangerously high. Another practice which is all too common and often seen in the summer at clay target shooting clubs when walking along the rows of cars parked in the blazing sun is to leave cartons of ammunition cooking – there is no other expression for this – in a closed car. Being placed inside the car on the sill immediately under and inside the back window, these cartridges are then, if in the full glare of the sun, probably being exposed to a temperature of $32\,°C$ plus. Although such storage can be dangerous some clay shooters deliberately leave their cartridge stored in their cars in the hot sun. They then reserve these hotted up cartridges for use in any shoot off in which they may be involved. This is a reprehensible practice and may be highly dangerous not only to the person shooting the cartridges but to any innocent competititor or bystander.

Damp conditions can cause paper cased cartridges to swell, making insertion and extraction very difficult. The roll crimps will almost certainly begin to unroll. When this occurs the strength of that particular roll crimp will be lessened which in turn will usually result in lowered pressures and pellet velocities, in fact erratic ballistics.

The importance of good firm consistent crimps cannot be overestimated, as cartridge makers and thinking sportsmen have always realized. Clay target shooters of my generation rightly make a practice of removing the unfired cartridge from their second barrel when they fire their first barrel and break their clay target. This unfired cartridge is then placed in the barrel they have just fired. It would then be the next cartridge to be fired, experience having taught us that it is unwise to fire a string of shots from the one barrel with the same unfired cartridge always sitting in the other barrel chamber being constantly exposed to the recoil. This constant firing of one barrel can have an effect and weaken the roll crimp on the unfired cartridge in the other barrel. DTL target shooting is a case in point: often in this discipline a top shooter will fire 100 cartridges from his first barrel and only one or two cartridges from his second barrel in the course of a 100-target shoot.

A few years ago there was quite an upsurge in the practice of reloading one's own cartridges. This reloading in turn brought in an increased number of examples of 'barrel pimpling'. The proof houses did some investigation into this phenomenon and the cause was found to be poor or weak crimping on these reloaded cartridges. (See Bibliography for the booklet *Notes on the Proof of Shotguns and other Small Arms* which is issued under the joint authority of our two proof houses. All sportsmen should for their own edification and safety own a copy of this booklet. They should carefully peruse and understand the facts it contains. Obtainable from either of the proof houses it is a most important publication as far as guns and shooters are concerned.)

Plastic cased cartridges are normally hardly affected by damp conditions and manufacturers' machine-made crimps on these new cartridges are usually excellent and consistently firm. Even so it is prudent to store cartridges as near as possible to the conditions advised by the manufacturers: these are 'cartridges should not be left exposed to the direct rays of the sun and at all times should be protected from extremes of temperature or humidity'.

## To Sum up the Use of the Card Rack

Measure all distances. Shoot only cartridges loaded with pellets of the same size and hardness when comparing cartridge performance. Only when the pellets are of the same hardness and size can one equate like with like. If the hardness of the shot varies between brands it is usual to find that the softer shot will penetrate fewer cards, the soft shot becoming more deformed as and when fired and due to being out of round the softer shot loses velocity plus penetration more quickly compared with the harder better-shaped pellets. Naturally the greater the distances at which tests are made the greater should be the differences between the performances of soft or hard shot. The advantages of soft shot arise when this shot in size 9 is used for skeet shooting. This is short range work at targets often travelling at narrow angles. Here the longer shot string of the soft shot helps. Also at the close ranges at which skeet targets are taken almost any small misshapen pellet will break the targets.

In fairness to the cartridge makers, they are well aware of the characteristics of hard or soft shot. Therefore when they produce a skeet cartridge the shot they choose will be soft. For live quarry or long distance targets they will use harder shot. There are many shooters who shoot well and happily, their creed being 'if I want a good skeet cartridge I go to my local expert in my usual gun shop and ask for whatever make of skeet cartridges they recommend. If I want an optimum performance wildfowling cartridge I go to my local gun shop; the manager in that shop periodically strips and cleans my gun, he knows the gun and will advise what cartridge he believes is best suited'. As long as the shooter has confidence in his gun shop the results should be good.

There are of course others who happily spend many hours reading up all the logistics. Then they will make up their own rack, do their own experiments from which they obtain much satisfaction. There are others who defy logic or reason, choosing their cartridges by either the colour of the cartridge case or the picture on the carton. All too often they are what the trade describe as 'straw clutchers', trying anything new and never staying with cartridge or gun long enough to settle down and produce a good performance. Each and every shooter must make his own choice as to what is best for him.

# 26

# Recoil and How to Tame it

## AMOUNT OF RECOIL

It has been calculated in the USA that the recoil from a 12 bore shotgun of $6\frac{1}{2}$ lb. when firing a normal cartridge can be in the order of 210 lb. This is a considerable amount of recoil to be transmitted into a shooter's shoulder pocket every time a cartridge is fired. Small wonder that coping with this recoil pressure time after time can be a traumatic experience for any shooter. Even when the gun is of full weight, with the recoil pad or gun butt correctly contoured to fit the owner's shoulder pocket, and when the shot load is compatible with the gun weight there will still be a limit to the number of cartridges any one person can fire without some after-effects. This limit will vary greatly between individuals.

Experts hold that the gun headache suffered by many after shooting is nothing more than mild concussion caused by the gun's recoil as and when each cartridge is fired. Be that as it may, and writing from the viewpoint of one who has been fortunate to suffer rarely from gun headache, it is a real problem for many. Some sufferers simply give up shooting. Others, more firmly addicted to the sport, will leave no stone unturned to find any palliative to alleviate their discomfort. There are many causes of shooting discomfort. Here are a few:

### Too Light a Gun Weight

This coupled with a cartridge which is incompatible due to too heavy a

211

shot load is one of the more obvious causes.

## An Ill-fitting Gun

This produces many problems. The butt plate may be the wooden end of the stock which may be badly shaped with its contours bearing no resemblance to the shape of the shoulder pocket.

## A Very Sharp Stock Toe

This is a common cause of discomfort. This combined with a straight stock with little cast at toe concentrates the recoil on a one square inch area of stock toe and shoulder flesh. The stock butt edges may be square and sharp. A combination of a long toe, sharp edges and little cast make it impossible for a broad-chested person of heavy build to mount such a stock correctly with barrels on a level plane. To enable such an ill-shape stocked gun to be fired in comfort inevitably results in the owner canting the gun allowing the butt to lie at an angle from the top of the shoulder pocket with the toe facing outwards and lying under the armpit. It is true there are those who by much practice can produce good scores with their guns so ill-mounted. But it is far better to have the gun fitter provide the shooter with a set of stock measurements which allow the fitted butt to be mounted comfortably with the barrels uncanted and precisely pointed. A badly shaped screw or stick-on butt pad will produce similar problems.

## A Narrow Stock Comb

This type of comb when used by someone who slam bangs the butt into his shoulder, often dropping his head at the same time, can result in facial abuse. Those with little flesh on the face will often find the forward end of the cheek-bone so badly bruised that a blood blister is formed at that point. The further forward the head and cheek is tipped the less flesh is available to take the recoil. A stock with excessive drop or bend is more likely to produce this cheek bruising.

## Recoil Pads

Much time and thought has gone into the production of soft recoil pads which help to soak up the recoil and firmly position the butt in the shoulder. Three very efficient recoil pads are the Parker Hale Pachmayre decelerator, the Morgan Adjustable and the Nickerson Sorbothane. These pads do require expert fitting. All too often one sees botched efforts at pad fitting when attending clay shoots. As for the game and live quarry shooter, the Silvers red rubber pad was customary wear for many years on the better class of game or wildfowling gun stock. These pads

Here is a well-built shooter with a gun which has had the butt contoured
to fit his shoulder pocket. The whole area of the butt is in contact with
the shooter's shoulder with recoil transmitted over the full area of the
pad into the shoulder in a straight line

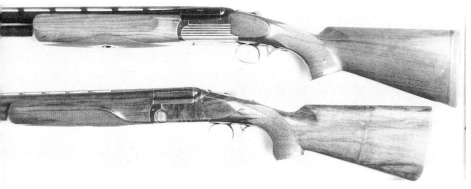

The gun below is the gun used in the illustration above.
Note the very short toe compared with the normal
toe on the gun above

also required careful fitting. Some shooters will find any of the above pads tend to drag as the butt is being slid up into the shoulder during gun mounting. The British gun trade as usual have had the complete answer for years. Their stock experts take a Silver type rubber pad and cover this with a piece of soft glove leather which covers all the end and sides of the pad. The finished article certainly expedites smooth gun mounting and soaks up recoil. Others have the Decelerator type pads fitted and will have instructed their stocker to polish the sides and end surface of the pad to encourage smoother non-stick gun mounting. The ladies will appreciate a well-fitted pad even more than the men.

## Other Points to Check Regarding an Ill-fitting Stock

To short a stock results in the recoil driving back the trigger hand into the shooter's face and mouth causing bruising and headache. Too long a stock causes the gun to lie across the body with the butt mounted way out on the shoulder point or even into the shooter's biceps. If on the shoulder point or arm/shoulder juncture, there are delicate nerves in that area which are painful when hit. As for the biceps, the resulting bruises have to be seen and felt to be really appreciated.

Too thin a stock hand or grip, which may also be of unsuitable shape, makes it difficult to hold the gun in a firm locked up position. Consider a badly balanced gun. If the gun is too light forward the barrels will tend to come up before the stock, and vice versa. When a fitted gun has been acquired, erratic gun mounting can be another source of discomfort. Those, who as they mount the gun slam, bang the butt into shoulder and comb into cheek, pulling back with both hands as they fire, thus add to

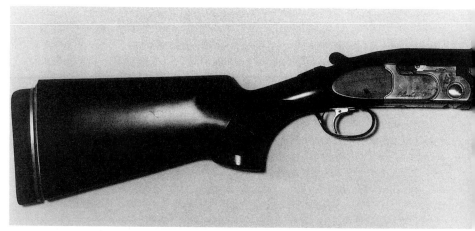

*A stock with a well-rounded adjustable recoil pad and a short toe. This pad can be angled to match shoulder pocket contours, which reduces felt recoil, muzzle flip and encourages recovery for that second shot*

the recoil. One should place, not slam the gun into the shoulder pocket. Pulling slightly backwards with the trigger hand while lightly pushing forward with the front hand transfers part of the recoil to the front hand and arm, reduces recoil and increases shooting comfort. The recovery time between first and second shots will be reduced.

## Body Balance and Weight Distribution

The weight should, wherever possible be slightly more on the front foot, with the shooter leaning into the recoil of the gun. The shooter's feet are his platform, upon which he balances in a comfortable position or stance. All of these factors have a bearing. Many shooters, due to their being given a heavy ill-fitting gun to commence shooting, have developed a 'lean back head up' stance. This laid back stance being aptly described by the CPSA coaching committee as 'going bananas'.

## Cartridges

The modern cartridge is a splendid article. Unfortunately many shooters insist on buying hot cartridges which they hope will assist them to 'get there fastest with the mostest'. These people all too often saddle themselves with cartridges producing excessive recoil. Not only must the cartridge shot load be compatible, but also the length of the cartridge case should be compatible with the chamber lengths of the gun barrels. Some of our makers of 'best' guns do have and for many years have had their named cartridges specially made so that when the pie crimp of the cartridge opens the length of the uncrimped cartridge case correctly matches the chamber of the gun. If a case is too long when uncrimped the crimp will obtrude into the barrel proper. This increases recoil. This is due to the shot charge and the wads having to be squeezed through a smaller hole than normal, the increased pressures encouraging more shot malformation plus poor ejection of the fired cases.

## Recoil Reducers

These fitments are popular in America and becoming increasingly so in Great Britain. One such is the Edwardes recoil reducer. This reducer consists of a small metal cylinder with a spring loaded weight inside. The stock is drilled to take the reducers. One or two reducers can be fitted into these stock holes. They are also adjustable to enable one to alter the direction of the recoil. Turning the reducer one way in its hole in the stock will encourage the recoil to be channelled away from the face and shoulder and vice versa. The addition of even dead weight to a gun reduces felt recoil. Experiments comparing the addition of a lead plug in the stock cavity with a recoil reducer of the same weight prove that the

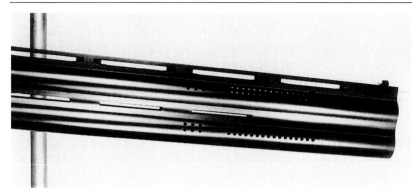

**Winchester barrel porting. This reduces recoil and barrel flip**

principle of these reducers is correct and felt recoil is reduced for the owner by their installation.

## OTHER METHODS OF REDUCING RECOIL

### Barrel Porting

Gun barrels are ported or drilled with many small holes; these holes are of special shape and angle. When the gun is fired the special holes direct hot jets of burning powder fumes outwards in such a manner that both recoil and barrel flip of the gun is reduced.

### Overboring

This system of increasing the internal diameter of the gun barrels by overboring by maybe $\frac{15}{1000}$ in is popular in the USA. Obviously it is easier to push a column of shot and wadding through a larger hole than a small one. Barrels which are overbored and barrel ported do seem to produce less felt recoil. Barrel porting certainly works for me. I once owned a semi-automatic gun with various barrels. One particular barrel was overbored $\frac{18}{1000}$ in British proofed at .740 in; it was also pro ported. All who test fired the gun agreed this gun seemed to produce less recoil than the norm. If a barrel is overbored, which results in the gun being 'out of proof', that barrel will have to be submitted and pass proof before it can be sold or used in this country. It would indeed be rare that any s/s gun would have barrels which were thick enough to be overbored. As a rule it is only pump or semi-automatic barrels which are thick enough to stand overboring.

## The Case for the Semi-Automatic Shotgun

It is well known by those who use semi-automatic guns for shooting or coaching that the recoil felt by the shooter feels less weight for weight than that produced by the traditional s/s or o/u: the reason being that gun recoil is transferred into the shoulder pocket during a longer period of time. This is due to the bolt being pushed rearwards in the action as soon as the cartridge is fired. This long push rearward spreads the time during which the recoil is transmitted into the shooter's shoulder. Modern semi-automatic guns utilize the burning powder gas pressure to move the bolt rearwards.

The majority of shooters find this longer push more acceptable to their shoulders than the short sharp recoil as produced by traditional guns. Many shooters claim less barrel flip when shooting the semi-automatic, and that this allows quicker recovery for their second shot. Every shooter should try the various combinations of differing gun types and cartridge until the felt recoil on the body and shoulder coupled with their shooting performance provides them with the best combination to suit their particular needs. In other words it depends on the individual's body and only he can really decide what suits him best.

## OTHER FACTORS

Some find excessive noise will seemingly produce for them a greater sensation of recoil. The remedy for such people is to wear well-fitted muffs.

Powder fumes, if inhaled, can cause headache and nausea similar to that caused by recoil. Some powder fumes are worse than others. Sore aching eyes are also a product of these fumes.

Protection of the shooter's shoulder pocket by means of shooting vests with special padding is essential. Some vests or jackets have fixed-on shoulder patches; others have pockets inside the vest shoulders which allow one to insert an anti-recoil pad. The shooter is spoilt for choice as far as shooting vests are concerned, and it is up to each individual to experiment until he finds something which suits his needs.

Experience has shown the majority of shooters become more susceptible to recoil by the time they are 40 years of age. Some only suffer physical discomfort; others complain that their 'trigger pulls go hard'. This is the shooter's twitch or flinch. This is dealt with in Chapter 14.

Therefore it seems that recoil can cause many problems with each shooter producing his own personal ones. As maintained throughout this book, the place to resolve such problems is at a shooting school in the company of a gun fitter-coach. As always, the fitter-coach will only alter one thing at any one time, then carefully check the shooter's reactions; to make many alterations at one and the same time will usually cause muddle without correct answers to a problem.

It is far better to make haste slowly by making carefully considered single alterations and checking these one at a time. Even when everything has been 'got right', a change of diet or illness may alter the body weight and gun fit. Shooting in light summer clothes can alter stock fitting, the variables are many and the remedies innumerable. Few mature shooters have not had problems with recoil, sometimes the cause is only in the shooter's imagination, but it is nevertheless very real to that person and must be exorcised. Overshooting, especially when tired or worried, can be a prime factor in building up recoil consciousness.

As usual there is no magic potion, no short cut, no gimmick; only plenty of controlled experiments to establish cause, effect and the most suitable gear which will produce an amount of recoil acceptable for that particular person. If and when this has been established and the best equipment acquired the onus is on the owner to make best use of it by constantly 'working on it'.

# 27
# Do-it-yourself Gun Repairs

YEARS ago it was alleged that Mr Punch was asked by a young man for advice on marriage. The reply was terse and to the point *'Don't'*. Whether Mr Punch was right or not is not for me to say. I am however very certain that most lay people who are contemplating doing their own gun repairs would be well advised to leave this highly skilled work to their gunsmith. A few examples may give the unbelievers, and there will be many, food for thought.

## Fitting New Firing Pins

A simple job indeed thinks the layman. It is true that with some modern guns which are made to close tolerances it may be perfectly possible to buy a replacement firing pin, slip off the stock and after controlling and removing the main spring(s) remove the old pin and replace it with another. This is fine – sometimes. The layman comes into the gun shop and wishes to buy a firing pin for his shotgun. The first thing the man in the shop wishes to know is whether the gun in question to be repaired is 'in proof'. Normally the customer 'believes' that his gun is in proof. In fact what many are really stating is that 'they hope it is'. Something quite different. Without gauges and the true knowledge even a qualified gunsmith will refuse to pronounce on a strange gun. Suppose the gunsmith out of the kindness of his heart has a replacement firing pin and sells this to the layman. If that gun is out of proof and subsequently blows up in shooting, the kind hearted gunsmith may have connived at repairing an out-of-proof gun. If the owner or a friend then suffers damage the possibilities are great. Gunsmiths undertake repairs to out-of-proof guns only if they can then prepare and submit the gun to proof. Until this happens and the gun passes, the owner will not be allowed to have the gun returned. If the gun blows up in proof the owner is still liable for the cost of repairs and any preparation for proof.

## Firing Pin Replacement

The gunsmith will replace a firing pin after he has checked the gun's condition. When the new pin is fitted a shotgun firing tester will be used to check the shape and the depth of the firing pin strike. It is not unknown for replacement firing pins to be too long. When this occurs the pin may be protruding too far out of the action face and cause the gun to fire as the gun is closed. Even if this does not happen, a too long pin may penetrate the percussion cap on the cartridge being fired. This can allow a jet of hot gases to come out of the hole in the cap and this jet can cause a cratered firing pin very quickly.

## Replacement Mainsprings

Again a seemingly simple matter. Springs do vary in strength. I knew one gentleman who lost a major championship due to the fact he replaced the mainspring for his bottom barrel the night before the shoot. The old coil mainspring had 'set' a little, and therefore the trigger pull was also on the easy side. A gunsmith would have found out what strength or poundage of pull the customer required and altered either the sear or bent or maybe even found a new spring of slightly differing strength. The owner went to the shoot and found out too late that the pull was around 8 lb. instead of its usual $3\frac{1}{2}$ lb. This so messed up his timing that, to use his own expression, 'he dropped a bucketfull'.

## Removing Dents in Barrels and Repolishing

The advent of the hydraulic dent raiser was hailed by some laymen as the complete answer to dents and their removal. There is nothing wrong with a hydraulic dent raiser when correctly used by an expert. But gun barrel walls are very thin, maybe 25 thousandths of an inch thick in some places. A few extra careless strokes on the dent raiser pumping mechanism and a dent can be quickly turned into a bulge. A good barrelsmith can put down bulges, but better they had never been produced. The gun trade has seen many dented barrels which have been reduced to scrap metal due to hydraulic dent raisers being inserted, pumped up on a dent, then brute force used to turn the tool in the barrel, resulting in a ruined barrel.

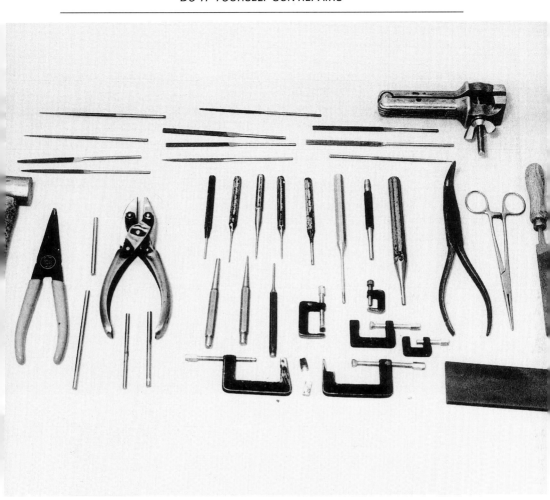

*A very small portion from a gunsmith's tool kit. Hammer with phosphor bronze head, fine jawed pliers, parallel-jawed pliers, slave pins, pin punches both parallel and pointed, fine files, hand vice, bent nose pliers, spring cramps of various shapes, forceps, carborundum slip stone*

## Valuation of Guns

It is not unknown for an owner to request a certificate of valuation to enable him to insure his gun. This is prudent. But there are three valuations, one is for replacement value in case the gun is stolen or wrecked in some way or another, the second is what the gun is worth for sale privately and the third is what the gun shop owner will pay in either a trade up or a straight cash sale.

Gun shops cannot continue in business unless they make a profit. If they buy a used gun they will strip and clean it before they put it up for resale. Gunsmith work is highly skilled and costs per hour are similar to that paid in the skilled motor repair trade. The cost of even a few hours work plus the gun shop's normal profit will have to be added to the buying in price of a gun when priced for resale. To produce a valuation certificate for any of the above reasons takes time and must cost money. But in case of theft or damage will prove money well spent. These days 'best' guns which have been owned even for a few years are usually under-insured. The prudent owner will have his guns revalued each year when they are given their usual strip and clean.

A gunsmith-maintained gun should be a safe gun. The owner should keep it safe when not in use. When in use muzzle awareness must be cultivated always. We are all fallible so 100 per cent care is always required. Regardless of what has been written, there will be those who are keen and determined to do their own thing, stripping down their own guns as and when they decide. For those people it is suggested a study of the books on stripping down guns will be worthwhile. (See Bibliography.)

## The Amateur's Tools

Turnscrews which fit the screw pins on the gun are essential. These are readily available from gun shops. It is standard gunsmith practice that any turnscrew bit will be contoured to match the slot of the screw pin to be removed. These slots are or should be well cut with square sides and bottoms. Some of the imported guns have extremely narrow slots. Do not do what some amateurs do, which is to file these slots wider. There was an instance of one gentleman who did this. Eventually he made the screw pin slots so wide that when he applied pressure with his fitted turnscrew he split the head of the screw. Most guns do have springs which are under tension or pressure; it is up to anyone working on any gun to keep these springs under control. It is also well worthwhile wearing protective shatterproof glasses at the same time. Some screw pins may be left handed and others right handed. Each pin should be returned to its original hole. The original pins are usually carefully fitted to enable all the screw head slots to lie in one direction.

## Stock Work

Another highly skilled occupation. Most stockers have their own formulae for stock finish; some will even sell a bottle of this to a customer. Having bought a bottle do not be surprised if the results are inferior to those obtained by the stocker. He has spent a lifetime on stocks; the secret of good stock finish lies mostly in the preparation of the wood surface and will take many hours.

*The work of a gunsmith is highly skilled and the expertise is not easily acquired*

## Barrel Blacking

An even more hazardous and highly skilled form of gun work. The formulae for obtaining that deep lustre black are many. Some may contain harmful chemicals. As with other gun work it is the preparation plus the application which counts. The reader will please himself; for myself I have always been prepared to pay someone else to do this. Any gun work they attempt is at their own risk. In case of even the slightest doubt one should always seek professional advice before any work is attempted; readers you have been warned.

# 28
# Conclusion

THERE is a certain small amount of repetition in this book. This has been done deliberately. I believe that it is better to repeat and stress the importance of key facets of gun handling especially when discussing the safe and the harmonious use of the gun, than to leave such points hidden in another chapter where they may be overlooked by the reader. As coaches and gun shop employees well know a gun can be on occasions a strange and frightening tool to some new owners. Therefore most believe that it is better to stress a point almost too often rather than mention it once and hope the gist has been fully understood by the client.

The usefulness of this book depends on the premise that the majority of human beings with normal coordination, eyesight, and with enough physical strength to handle a shotgun can be taught how to shoot safely, if they are prepared to apply themselves fully to this purpose.

In an ideal world the gun will fit the shooter; all too often it is the shooter who has to fit himself to the gun. This state of affairs is up to the shooter. Anyone with cash and the will to succeed should be able eventually to obtain a gun fitted to suit himself and for whatever purpose the gun is required.

Any coach worthy of the name will prescribe a set of exercises which if practised for a few minutes every day ensures muscle memory and consistent gun mounting, which is the secret of safe good shooting. The gun must be in sound shootable condition, with suitable borings and compatible ammunition. Gun safety and muzzle awareness *must* be cultivated until regardless or not whether the gun is loaded the muzzles are always under control and pointed in a safe direction at all times. If there is doubt regarding the safety of any shot, that shot should *not* be taken. Putting the pellet pattern on the target, one shoots a moving target with a moving gun; experience has proved to most coaches that, given good mounting with a fitted gun, most misses are low and behind. Those clients whose leads err on the long side are usually the better performers.

Once a good combination of cartridge and gun is established, stick to that combination regardless of any minor hiccups. At times, there will be less than good days; forget them and concentrate on the good days to such an effect that you can repeat them.

## Good Shooting

It is important to understand that safe shooting depends on the manner in which the gun is handled. This is up to the shooter. It is his finger on the trigger, and his control of the gun point.

# Appendix 1
# Useful Tables

## USEFUL TABLES

1 Details of shot sizes; comparison with other countries
2 Number of pellets in shot load
3 Patterns at all ranges
4 Diameter of spread
5 Striking energy for individual pellets
6 Eley's shotgun cartridge

All the following tables and illustrations are courtesy of Eley.

# 1 DETAILS OF SHOT SIZES

| | Details of Shot Sizes (nominal) | | | | | | Comparison of Shot Sizes (approximations only) | | | | | | | |
|---|---|---|---|---|---|---|---|---|---|---|---|---|---|---|
| Design | Pellets | | Weight per pellet | | Diameter | | English | Canadian | American* | French | Belgian | Italian | Dutch | Spanish |
| | per oz. | per 10g | grains | g | in | mm | | | | | | | | |
| LG | 6 | 2 | 70·00 | 4·54 | ·36 | 9·1 | LG | — | — | — | — | — | — | — |
| SG | 8 | 3 | 54·70 | 3·54 | ·33 | 8·4 | SG | SSG | ooBuck | — | 9G | 11/0 | 9G | — |
| Spec. SG | 11 | 4 | 39·77 | 2·58 | ·30 | 7·6 | Spec. SG | SG | 1 Buck | C2 | 12G | 9/0 | 12G | — |
| SSG | 15 | 5½ | 29·17 | 1.89 | ·27 | 6·8 | SSG | AAAA | 3 Buck | C3 | — | — | — | — |
| AAA | 35 | 12½ | 12·50 | 0·81 | ·20 | 5·2 | AAA | AAA | 4 Buck | 5/0 | — | — | — | — |
| BB | 70 | 25 | 6·25 | 0·40 | ·16 | 4·1 | BB | Air rifle | Air rifle | 1 | oo | oo | oo | 1 |
| 1 | 100 | 36 | 4·38 | 0·28 | ·14 | 3·6 | 1 | 2 | 2 | 3 | — | 1 or 2 | — | 3 |
| 3 | 140 | 50 | 3·12 | 0·20 | ·13 | 3·3 | 3 | 4 | 4 | 4 | — | 3 | — | 4 |
| 4 | 170 | 60 | 2·57 | 0·17 | ·12 | 3·1 | 4 | 5 | 5 | 5 | — | 4 | — | 5 |
| 5 | 220 | 78 | 1·99 | 0·13 | ·11 | 2·8 | 5 | 6 | 6 | 6 | 5 | 5 | 5 | 6 |
| 6 | 270 | 95 | 1·62 | 0·10 | ·10 | 2·6 | 6 | — | — | — | 6 | 6 | 6 | — |
| 7 | 340 | 120 | 1·29 | 0·08 | ·095 | 2·4 | 7 | 7½ | 7½ | 7 | 7 | 7½ | 7 | 7 |
| 7½ | 400 | 140 | 1·12 | 0·07 | ·09 | 2·3 | 7½ | 8 | 8 | 7½ | 7½ | 8 | 7½ | 7½ |
| 8 | 450 | 160 | 0·97 | 0·06 | ·085 | 2·2 | 8 | — | — | 8 | 8 | — | 8 | 8 |
| 9 | 580 | 210 | 0·75 | 0·05 | ·08 | 2·0 | 9 | 9 | 9 | 9 | 9 | 9½ | 9 | 9 |

g = grams
* also Swedish

## 2 NUMBER OF PELLETS IN SHOT LOAD

(nominal)

| Weight of shot | | Size of shot | | | | | |
|---|---|---|---|---|---|---|---|
| g | oz. | 3 | 4 | 5 | 6 | 7 | 8 |
| 46 | $1\frac{5}{8}$ | 228 | 276 | 358 | 439 | 552 | 732 |
| 42·5 | $1\frac{1}{2}$ | 210 | 255 | 330 | 405 | 510 | 675 |
| 36 | $1\frac{1}{4}$ | 175 | 213 | 275 | 338 | 425 | 562 |
| 34 | $1\frac{3}{16}$ | 166 | 202 | 261 | 321 | 404 | 534 |
| 32 | $1\frac{1}{8}$ | 157 | 191 | 248 | 304 | 383 | 506 |
| 30 | $1\frac{1}{16}$ | 149 | 181 | 234 | 287 | 361 | 478 |
| 28·5 | 1 | 140 | 170 | 220 | 270 | 340 | 450 |
| 26·5 | $\frac{15}{16}$ | 131 | 159 | 206 | 253 | 319 | 422 |
| 25 | $\frac{7}{8}$ | 122 | 149 | 193 | 326 | 298 | 394 |
| 23 | $\frac{13}{16}$ | 113 | 138 | 179 | 219 | 276 | 366 |
| 17·5 | $\frac{5}{8}$ | 87 | 106 | 138 | 169 | 212 | 282 |
| 16 | $\frac{9}{16}$ | 78 | 96 | 124 | 152 | 191 | 254 |
| 12·5 | $\frac{7}{16}$ | 61 | 75 | 97 | 118 | 149 | 187 |
| 9 | $\frac{5}{16}$ | 44 | 53 | 69 | 84 | 106 | 141 |

# 3 PATTERNS AT ALL RANGES

It is possible to calculate the number of pellets in a 75 cm (30 in) circle for any shot size and in any of the six borings of gun at the ranges stated, by using table 2 (total pellets in the charge) and the following table.

**Percentage of total pellets in 75 cm circle**

| Boring of Gun | Range in metres | | | | | | | |
|---|---|---|---|---|---|---|---|---|
| | 20 | 25 | 30 | 35 | 40 | 45 | 50 | 55 |
| True Cyl. | 75 | 63 | 53 | 43 | 35 | 28 | 22 | 18 |
| Imprvd. Cyl. | 85 | 74 | 64 | 53 | 43 | 34 | 27 | 22 |
| $\frac{1}{4}$-Choke | 90 | 80 | 70 | 58 | 48 | 39 | 31 | 25 |
| $\frac{1}{2}$-Choke | 97 | 86 | 76 | 64 | 54 | 43 | 34 | 27 |
| $\frac{3}{4}$-Choke | 100 | 93 | 83 | 70 | 58 | 47 | 38 | 30 |
| Full Choke | 100 | 100 | 90 | 74 | 62 | 51 | 41 | 32 |

**Percentage of total pellets in 30 in circle**

| Boring of Gun | Range in yards | | | | | | | | |
|---|---|---|---|---|---|---|---|---|---|
| | 20 | 25 | 30 | 35 | 40 | 45 | 50 | 55 | 60 |
| True Cyl. | 80 | 69 | 60 | 49 | 40 | 33 | 27 | 22 | 18 |
| Imprvd. Cyl. | 92 | 82 | 72 | 60 | 50 | 41 | 33 | 27 | 22 |
| $\frac{1}{4}$-Choke | 100 | 87 | 77 | 65 | 55 | 46 | 38 | 30 | 25 |
| $\frac{1}{2}$-Choke | 100 | 94 | 83 | 71 | 60 | 50 | 41 | 33 | 27 |
| $\frac{3}{4}$-Choke | 100 | 100 | 91 | 77 | 65 | 55 | 46 | 37 | 30 |
| Full Choke | 100 | 100 | 100 | 84 | 70 | 59 | 49 | 40 | 32 |

*Example:* Charge 30 g ($1\frac{1}{16}$ oz.) No. 6; find pattern at 40 yards for a half-choke barrel. Total pellets: 287 multiplied by 60 (from the table above) and divided by 100. Answer 172.

## 4 DIAMETER OF SPREAD

Diameter in inches and centimetres covered by the bulk of the charge of a cartridge at various ranges for all calibres according to the degree of choke of the gun.

**Centimetres**

| Boring of Gun | Range in metres | | | | | |
|---|---|---|---|---|---|---|
| | 10 | 15 | 20 | 25 | 30 | 35 |
| True Cyl. | 54 | 71 | 88 | 105 | 122 | 140 |
| Imprvd. Cyl. | 38 | 55 | 72 | 89 | 106 | 124 |
| $\frac{1}{4}$-Choke | 34 | 49 | 64 | 80 | 97 | 115 |
| $\frac{1}{2}$-Choke | 31 | 44 | 58 | 73 | 90 | 108 |
| $\frac{3}{4}$-Choke | 27 | 39 | 52 | 66 | 82 | 101 |
| Full Choke | 23 | 33 | 45 | 59 | 75 | 94 |

**Inches**

| Boring of Gun | Range in yards | | | | | | |
|---|---|---|---|---|---|---|---|
| | 10 | 15 | 20 | 25 | 30 | 35 | 40 |
| True Cyl. | 20 | 26 | 32 | 38 | 44 | 51 | 58 |
| Imprvd. Cyl. | 15 | 20 | 26 | 32 | 38 | 44 | 51 |
| $\frac{1}{4}$-Choke | 13 | 18 | 23 | 29 | 35 | 41 | 48 |
| $\frac{1}{2}$-Choke | 12 | 16 | 21 | 26 | 32 | 38 | 45 |
| $\frac{3}{4}$-Choke | 10 | 14 | 18 | 23 | 29 | 35 | 42 |
| Full Choke | 9 | 12 | 16 | 21 | 27 | 33 | 40 |

# 5 STRIKING ENERGY FOR INDIVIDUAL PELLETS

(nominal)

## Metre kilogrammes

| Cartridge velocity level | Shot size | Range (metres) | | | | | |
|---|---|---|---|---|---|---|---|
| | | 20 | 25 | 30 | 35 | 40 | 45 |
| Trap Extra (322 m/sec) 1060 ft sec | 7 | 0·277 | 0·227 | 0·187 | 0·152 | 0·121 | 0·097 |
| | 8 | 0·197 | 0·161 | 0·131 | 0·102 | 0·084 | 0·061 |
| | BB | 1·65 | 1·48 | 1·34 | 1·17 | 1·04 | 0·93 |
| Standard Game (325 m/sec) 1070 ft sec | 3 | 0·762 | 0·660 | 0·574 | 0·494 | 0·425 | 0·368 |
| | 4 | 0·614 | 0·526 | 0·453 | 0·389 | 0·330 | 0·278 |
| | 5 | 0·462 | 0·391 | 0·330 | 0·276 | 0·232 | 0·192 |
| | 6 | 0·365 | 0·306 | 0·257 | 0·212 | 0·173 | 0·142 |
| | 7 | 0·281 | 0·233 | 0·192 | 0·155 | 0·126 | 0·101 |
| | 9 | 0·152 | 0·119 | 0·096 | 0·075 | 0·055 | 0·040 |
| High Velocity (340 m/sec) 1120 ft sec | 3 | 0·814 | 0·702 | 0·608 | 0·522 | 0·455 | 0·392 |
| | 4 | 0·652 | 0·561 | 0·482 | 0·411 | 0·350 | 0·297 |
| | 5 | 0·490 | 0·414 | 0·351 | 0·295 | 0·248 | 0·205 |
| | 6 | 0·387 | 0·327 | 0·271 | 0·227 | 0·187 | 0·153 |
| | 7 | 0·299 | 0·248 | 0·202 | 0·167 | 0·135 | 0·108 |

## Foot pounds

| Cartridge velocity level | Shot size | Range (yards) | | | | | |
|---|---|---|---|---|---|---|---|
| | | 20 | 30 | 35 | 40 | 45 | 50 |
| Trap Extra (322 m/sec) 1060 ft sec | 7 | 2·16 | 1·48 | 1·23 | 1·01 | 0·83 | 0·68 |
| | 8 | 1·53 | 1·03 | 0·84 | 0·68 | 0·54 | 0·43 |
| | BB | 12·4 | 10·3 | 9·24 | 8·25 | 7·38 | 6·56 |
| Standard Game (325 m/sec) 1070 ft sec | 3 | 5·79 | 4·48 | 3·92 | 3·43 | 2·99 | 2·59 |
| | 4 | 4·68 | 3·54 | 3·08 | 2·66 | 2·30 | 1·97 |
| | 5 | 3·52 | 2·60 | 2·23 | 1·90 | 1·61 | 1·36 |
| | 6 | 2·80 | 2·03 | 1·71 | 1·44 | 1·20 | 1·01 |
| | 7 | 2·16 | 1·52 | 1·27 | 1·06 | 0·86 | 0·70 |
| | 9 | 1·18 | 0·77 | 0·62 | 0·48 | 0·38 | 0·28 |
| High Velocity (340 m/sec) 1120 ft sec | 3 | 6·22 | 4·73 | 4·13 | 3·61 | 3·17 | 2·77 |
| | 4 | 4·99 | 3·75 | 3·28 | 2·85 | 2·45 | 2·11 |
| | 5 | 3·76 | 2·77 | 2·37 | 2·03 | 1·73 | 1·46 |
| | 6 | 2·98 | 2·15 | 1·84 | 1·55 | 1·30 | 1·08 |
| | 7 | 2·30 | 1·63 | 1·36 | 1·14 | 0·93 | 0·76 |

A rough guide to the minimum requirements for a clean kill is: Small birds – 2 pellets each of 0·07 m kg (0·5 ft lb) striking energy; Medium birds – 3 pellets each of 0·12 m kg (0·85 ft lb) striking energy; Large birds – 4 pellets each of 0·21 m kg (1·5 ft lb) striking energy.

# 6 ELEY'S SHOTGUN CARTRIDGE

# The shotgun cartridge

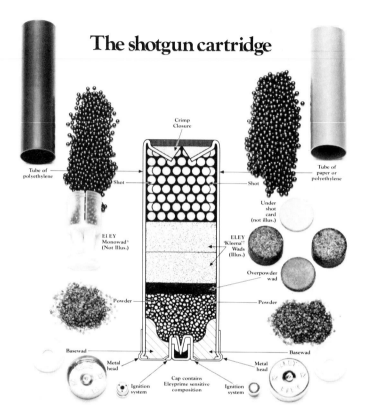

Crimp Closure

Tube of polyethylene

Shot

Shot

Tube of paper or polyethylene

Under shot card (not illus.)

ELEY Monowad* (Not Illus.)

ELEY 'Kleena' Wads (Illus.)

Overpowder wad

Powder

Powder

Basewad

Basewad

Metal head

Metal head

Ignition system

Cap contains Eleyprime sensitive composition

Ignition system

ELEY

*ELEY Monowad shot protector and main driving wad.

†ELEY 'Kleena' biodegradable main driving wads.

# Appendix 2
# Useful Addresses

## USEFUL ADDRESSES

British Association for Shooting and Conservation, Marford Mill, Rossett, Clwyd, LL12 0HL

British Field Sports Society, 59 Kennington Rd, London, SE1 7PZ

British Shooting Sports Council, Pentridge, Salisbury, SP5 5QX

Clay Pigeon Shooting Association, 107 Epping New Rd, Buckhurst Hill, Essex, IQ9 5TQ

The Game Conservancy, Fordingbridge, Hants

Institute of Clay Shooting Instructors, c/o Clay Pigeon Shooting Association

The Irish Clay Pigeon Shooting Association, 20 Butterfield Drive, Rathfarnham, Dublin 14

The Scottish Clay Pigeon Shooting Association, 2 Greengill, Gilcrux, Aspatria, Carlisle, Cumberland

The Ulster Clay Pigeon Shooting Association, 6 Springhill Avenue, Bangor, County Down

The Welsh Clay Target Shooting Association, 45 Picton Rd, Hakin, Milford Haven, Dyfed

### Proof Houses

Birmingham: The Birmingham Gun Barrel Proof House, Banbury St, Birmingham, B5 5RH

London: The Gunmakers Company, 48 Commercial Road, London, E1;

Shooting Sports Trust, 115 Psalter Lane, South Yorks, S11 8YR

The CPSA began their club coaches award scheme some years ago. This has proved very successful and to date there are more than 300 CPSA club coaches with a more than one year's waiting list. Clay shooting is booming as never before and the cpsa has now set up the Institute of Clay Shooting Instructors (icsi) to ensure that coaching standards are maintained and improved. To quote from the prospectus:

> The objects of the Institute shall be to further and foster the art and profession of clay pigeon shooting instruction by providing and maintaining proper standards of knowledge, ability and status for each class of membership as shall be determined from time to time by the Council of the Institute.

The membership grades are:
Honorary Fellow (Hon ficsi)
Fellow (ficsi)
Member (micsi)

I believe the objects of this institute are splendid and there will be many instructors and coaches endeavouring to join it.

# Bibliography

## BOOKS AND ARTICLES

Ackley, P.O., *Home Gun Care and Repair*, (1969)

Akehurst, R., *Game Guns and Rifles*, (1969)

Alington, C., *Partridge Driving*, (1904)

Allen, Capt. L., *Leaves from a Game Book*, (1946); *Rough Shoot*, (1942); *Shotgun & Sunlight*, (1951)

Angier, R.H., *Firearms Blueing & Browning*, (1936)

Anon, *The Art of Shooting Flying*, (c. 1785)

Arnold, R., *Shooters Handbook*, (1955); *Automatic and Repeating Shotguns*, (1958)

Arthur, R., *The Shotgun Stock*, (1971)

Askins, Col. Charles, sen., *Wing and Trap Shooting*, (1910); *The American Shotgun*, (1910); *Modern Shotguns and Loads*, (1929); *Game Bird Shooting*, (1931)

Askins, Col. Charles, jun., *Wing and Trap Shooting*, (1948); *Shotgunners Handbook*, (1958)

Badminton Library, *Shooting: Field and Covert*, (1886); *Shooting: Moor and Marsh*, (1893)

Badminton Magazine, *The Holland & Holland Shooting School*, (1896)

Bailey, De Witt & Nie, D.A., *English Gunmakers*, (1978)

Baker, Clyde, *Modern Gunsmithing*, (1933)

Baker, Max, *Sport with Woodpigeons*, (1934)

BASC., *A Handbook of Shooting*, (1983)

Bearse, R., *Sporting Arms of the World*, (1976)

Beaumont, R., *Purdey's, The Guns and the Family*, (1984)

Bentley, P., *Clay Target Shooting*, (1987)

Beresford, Hon C., *Beresford's Monte Carlo*, (c. 1910)

Birmingham Proof House, *A History*, (1946)

Blagdon, *Shooting*, (1900)

Bogardus, A.G., *Field, Cover and Trap Shooting*, (1881)

Bonnet, Frank, *Mixed and Rough Shooting*, (1914)

Blaines, *Rural Sports*, (1858)

Boughan, R., *Shotgun Ballistics*, (1965)

Boothroyd, G., *Gun Collecting*, (1961); *Shotguns and Gunsmiths, The Vintage Years*, (1986); *The Shotgun, History and Development*, (1985)

Briggs, E., *Shots Heard Around the World*, (1956)

Brindle, J., *Shotguns and Shooting*, (1984)

Brister, R., *Shotgunning, The Art & The Science*, (1976); *Moss, Mallards & Mules*, (1973)

Bromley-Davenport, W., *Sport*, (1888)

Broomfield, B. & Cradock, C., *Shotguns on Test*, (1980)

Brownell, B., *Encyclopedia of Modern Firearms*, (1959); *Gunsmith Kinks 1*, (1969); *Gunsmith Kinks 2*, (1983)

Browning, J. & Gentry, C., *J.M. Browning American Gunmaker*, (1982)

Bruette, W.A., *Guncraft*, (1912)

Burch, M., *Gun Care & Repair*, (1978)

Burrard, Maj. Sir Gerald, *In the Gunroom*, (1930); *The Modern Shotgun*, (3 vols), (1931)

Burrard, Sir Gerald, *Identification of Firearms*, (1934)

Buxton, A., *The King in his Country*, (1955)

Buxton, S., *Fishing & Shooting*, (1902)

Carmichael, J., *Gunsmithing: Do-It-Yourself*, (1977)

Cadieux, C.L., *Goose Hunting*, (1979)

Carey, L., *My Gun & I*, (1933)

Chapel, C.E., *Field Skeet and Trap Shooting*, (1949)

Churchill, R., *How to Shoot*, (1925); *Game Shooting*, (1955); *Churchill's Shotgun Book*, (1955)

Clapham, R., *Rough Shooting*, (1930); *The ABC of Shooting*, (1930)

Country Life Library, *Shooting* (2 vols), (1903)

Cradock, C., *A Manual of Clayshooting*, (1983)

Cradock, Lieut. R.N., *Sporting Notes in the Far East*, (1911)

Craige, J.H., *Practical Book of American Guns*, (1950)

Craven, R., *Recreations in Shooting*, (1846)

Crudgington, I. & Baker, D., *The British Shotgun*, (1979)

Curtis, P.A., *Guns and Gunning*, (1934)

Curtis & Harvey, *Notes on Shooting*, (1904)

Daniel, Revd. W.B., *Rural Sport* (2 vols), (1801)

Dawson, Maj. K., *Marsh & Mudflat*, (1931)

Day, Wentworth, J., *Sporting Adventure*, (1938); *Sport in Egypt*, (1938); *George Vth as a Sportsman*, (1935); *The Modern Fowler*, (1949); *The Modern Shooter*, (1952)

Dobson, W., *Kunopaedia: Art of Shooting Flying*, (1817)

Dobie, W.G.M., *Winter & Rough Weather*, (1938); *Game Bag & Creel*, (1927)

Dougall, J.D., *Shooting Simplified*, (1865)

Dunlap, R.F., *Gunsmithing*, (1963); *Gun Owners Book*, (1974)

Drought, J.B., *A Shot in the Making*, (1948); *Successful Shooting*, (1948)

Drydon, H.A., *Nature & Sport in Britain*, (1904)

East Sussex, *The Shotgun & its Uses*, (1914)

Eley, *Layouts for Clay Target Shooting*, (1971); *Shooting Technique with M. Rose*, (1978); *Eley Shooters Diary*, (Annual)

Escrit, L.B., *Rifle and Gun*, (1953)
Elliot, A. & G., *Gun Fun and Hints*, (1946)
Etchen, F., *Commonsense Shotgun Shooting*, (1946)
Expert, *Notes on Shooting*, (1915)
Forester, F., *Complete Manual for Young Sportsmen*, (1856)
Field Press, *Partridges*, (1927)
Garner, P., *Shotguns*, (1963)
Garrard, D., *Cartridge Loading*, (1978)
Garwood, Gough Thomas, *Shotguns & Cartridges*, (1963); *Gun Book*, (1969); *Shooting Facts & Fancies*, (1978)
Gladstone, H.S., *Record Bags & Shooting Records*, (1922); *Shooting with Surtees*, (1927)
Greener, W., *The Gun*, (1834)
Greener, W.W., *Modern Breechloaders*, (1871); *The Breechloader & How to Use It*, (1892); *Modern Shotguns*, (1888); *The Gun*, 9th ed., (1910)
Gunmakers Association, *Gun Sense*, (no date)
Gunmakers Co. and the Guardians of Birmingham Proof House, *Rules of Proof*, (1954)
Harrison, E., *Guns & Shooting*, (1908)
Hartman, B., *Hartman on Skeet*, (1967)
Hatchers, J.S., *Hatchers Notebook*, (1947)
Hawker, Col. P., *Instructions to Young Shooters*, (1833); *The Diary*, (1893)
Hearne, A., *Shooting & Gunfitting*, (1946)
Hinman, R., *Golden Age of Shotgunning*, (1971)
Holts, *Holts Shooting Calendar* (2 vols), (1882–3)
Hood, A., *Shooting*, (1909)
Howe, J., *The Modern Gunsmith* (2 vols), (1934)
Humphreys, J., *The Shooting Handbook* (2 vols), (1984–5); *Learning to Shoot*, (1985)
ICI, *The Stringing of Shot*, (1926)
Jennings, M., *Instinct Shooting*, (1965)
Johnson, P., *The Parker Gun*, (1961)
Joint Authority of the Worshipful Company of Gunmakers of the City of London and the Guardians of the Birmingham Proof House, *Notes on the Proof of Shotguns & other Small Arms*, (1960, 1976, 1981)
Keith, E., *Shotguns*, (1950)
Keith, E.C., *Gun for Company*, (1937)
Kennedy, M., *Checkering and Carving Gunstocks*, (1952)
King, P., *The Shooting Field, Holland & Holland*, (1985)
Kynoch, *Shooting Notes & Comments*, (1910)
Lancaster, *Art of Shooting*, (1889)
Lavin, I., *History of Spanish Firearms*, (1965)
Lee, B., *Trap Shooting*, (1969); *Skeet Shooting*, (1969)
Lennox, Lord W., *Recreations of a Sportsman* (2 vols), (1862)
Lind, E., *Complete Book of Trick Shooting*, (1972)
Long, W.H.T., *The Gun in the Field*, (no date)
Lonsdale Library, Parker, E., (ed.), *Shooting*, (1929); *Shooting Records*, (1929); *The Keepers Book*, (1929); *Wildfowling*, (1929); *Game Birds & Beasts*, (1929)
Macintyre, D., *Memories of a Highland Gamekeeper*, (1926)
Mackie, Sir P., *The Keepers Book*, (1910)
Marchington, J., *The Complete Shot*, (1981); *Book of Shotguns*, (1984)

Marksman, *The Dead Shot*, (1860)

McFarland, F., *Clay Pigeon Shooting*, (1964)

Maxwell, A., *Grouse and Grouse Moors*, (1910); *Partridges & Partridge Manors*, (1911); *Pheasants & Covert Shooting*, (1913)

Migdalski, E., *Clay Target Games*, (1978)

Mills & Barnes, *Amateur Gunsmithing*, (1986)

Misseldine, F., *Skeet & Trap Shooting*, (1968)

Money, A.W., (Blue Rock), *Pigeon Shooting*, (1987)

Montague, A., *Successful Shotgun Shooting*, (1971)

Moreton, *et al.*, *Gun Talk*, (1973)

Newell, D., *Gunstock Finishing & Care*, (1949)

Nicholls, J., *Shooting Ways*, (no date)

Nicholls, R., *Skeet*, (1939); *The Shotgunner*, (1949)

Nobel Industries, *The Versatile Clay Bird*, (1921); *A Handbook of Clay Target Shooting*, (1927)

Oberfell & Thompson, *Mysteries of Shotgun Patterns*, (1960)

Old Gamekeeper, *Shooting on the Wing*, (1884)

Parker, E., *Elements of Shooting*, (1924)

Payne-Gallwey, R., *Letters to Young Shooters*, (3 vols), (1895–1914); *High Pheasants: Theory & Practice*, (1913)

Petrel, *Approach to Shooting*, (1954)

Pollard, H., *Shotguns*, (1923); *History of Firearms*, (1926); *Gamebirds & Game Bird Shooting*, (1926); *Gunroom Guide*, (1930)

Pollard, H. & Barclay Smith, P., *British & American Game Birds*, (1945)

Purdey, T. & J., *The Shotgun*, (1936)

Purple Heather, *Something About Guns & Shooting*, (1891)

Raymont, M., *Modern Clay Pigeon Shooting*, (1974)

Reynolds, M. & Barnes, M., *Shooting Made Easy*, (1986)

Riling, R., *Guns & Shooting*, (1951)

Ruffer, J.E.M., *Art of Good Shooting*, (1976)

Sedgewick, N., *The Young Shot*, (1940)

Sell, F., *Surehit Shotgun Ways*, (1967)

Service, *Shooting*, (no date)

Shand, *The Gun Room*, (no date)

Sharp, R., *The Gun*, (1903); *Modern Sporting Gunnery*, (1906)

Shooting Sports Trust, *Buying a Shotgun*, (1981)

Spearing, G.W., *The Craft of the Gunsmith*, (1986)

Smith, L., *Trap Shooting*, (1925); *Modern Shotgun Shooting*, (1935); *Shotgun Psychology*, (1938)

Sporting Arms, *Handbook on Shotgun Shooting*, (1940)

Stack, R., *Shotgun Digest*, (1974)

Stanbury, P. & Carlisle, G., *Shotgun Marksmanship*, (1962); *Clay Pigeon Marksmanship*, (1962); *Shotgun and Shooter*, (1970)

Stonehenge, *The Sporting Gun*, (1859)

Teasdale-Buckell, G. T., *Experts on Guns & Shooting*, (1900); *The Complete Shot*, (1907); *Land and Water*, (1889)

Twenty Bore, *Practical Hints on Shooting*, (1887)

Wagner, F., *Art of Shooting*, (1926)

Wallack, L., *American Shotgun Design*, (1977)

Walsh, *Rural Sports*, (1881); *Modern Sportsman's Gun*, (1882)

Walsh, H., *Outlaw Gunner*, (1971)

Watt, *Remarks on Shooting in Verse*, (1839)
Wilson, J., *Oakleigh Shooting Code*, (1837)
Winsberger, *Standard Directory of Proof Marks*, (1975)
Zutz, D., *The Double Shotgun*, (1987)

## *VIDEO FILMS*

*Game Shooting* Holland & Holland/Shooting Times
*Sporting Clay Shooting* Holland & Holland/Shooting Times
*Sporting Clays* B. Hebditch, B. Simpson, narrator M. Barnes, Gunmark
*The Sporting Shotgun* J. Douglas & C. Cradock
*Sporting Shotgun Shooting* J. Douglas & P. Bentley
*Trap Shooting with Lee Braun*, Remington/Hull Cartridge
*Skeet Shooting with Lee Braun*, Remington/Hull Cartridge

## *BRITISH MAGAZINES*

*Country Sport* (monthly)
*The Field* (monthly)
*Guns Review* (monthly)
*Shooting Gazette* (quarterly)
*Pull* (bimonthly)
*Shooting Times* (weekly)
*Shooting Magazine* (monthly)
*Sporting Gun* (monthly)
*Shooting Life* (monthly)

## *AMERICAN MAGAZINES*

*American Rifleman* (monthly)
*Field & Stream* (monthly)
*Guns & Ammo* (monthly)
*Sporting Clays*
*American Annuals*
*Gun Digest*
*Guns & Ammo*
*Shooters Bible*

# Glossary and Abbreviations

**ABT** Automatic Ball Trap

**Action** The body of a gun containing most of the moving parts. May be boxlock or sidelock with single or double barrel, or single barrel semi-automatic, pump, or Martini action. Assuming equal qualities of workmanship and materials the conventionally designed sidelock double hammerless ejector has more moving parts and usually costs more to produce.

**Action bolt** A steel bolt which fits into the bite of the barrel lump and holds action and barrel together.

**Action top strap** A piece of steel usually integral with the action and placed at the rear end of it.

**Action bottom strap** A piece of metal which may or may not be integral with the action and placed at the bottom rear end of it.

**Anson & Deeley** A boxlock action designed by Messrs Anson & Deeley, introduced in 1875. Even today the majority of modern actions are broadly based on this design.

**Barrel** The steel tube complete with lump, etc., in the chamber of which a suitable cartridge can be placed and fired, the pellets being discharged up and out through the muzzle.

**Barrels** Two steel tubes fastened together by various methods, in which suitable cartridges can be placed as above for the same purpose.

**Barrel flats** Usually in a side by side gun the breech ends of the barrels are flat where they sit on the action table.

**Barrel selector** Usually a catch, lever, or small button fitted to a single selective trigger double gun. Movement of this selector allows the shooter to choose which barrel he fires first.

**BASC** British Association for Shooting and Conservation. Founded in 1908 by Stanley Duncan as 'The Wildfowlers Association of Great Britain and Ireland'.

**Bent** A notch in the hammer or tumbler into which the sear nose fits when the gun is cocked.

**Bifurcated** As applied to the jointing of a gun, means two. A trunnion is placed on each side of the barrel replacing the one solid hinge pin underneath, resulting in a shallower action.

**Bite(s)** Notch(es) in the barrel lump(s), into which the bolt(s) engage.

**Blacking** A chemically produced black finish as applied to barrels, actions, etc.

**Bolt** *See* **Action bolt**

**Bore/gauge** The inside diameter of a barrel. The bore size or diameter for proof is measured 9 in from the breech. This diameter is based on the number of pure lead spherical balls each fitting the bore, which go to the English 16 oz. pound. A 12 bore gun would therefore accept 12 spherical balls, which weighed together would equal one pound. This holds true for all bores except the .410 calibre, which is shown in decimals of an inch as .410.

**Boxlock** A box shaped action containing internal lockwork, very different from a sidelock whose locks are on the insides of the lock plates.

**Breech** The end of the barrel into which a cartridge is inserted.

**Calibre** *See* **Bore/gauge**

**Calling one's shots** Knowing why and where one has missed a target.

**Cartridge** *See* Appendix 1, fig. 6 showing Eley cartridges and components.

**Case hardening** A process whereby the outer skin or casing of the action and other parts are hardened. It may be done chemically. In Britain it is usually achieved by packing the parts in a steel pot in a mixture of, basically, ground bones and leather scraps. The whole is heated and then allowed to cool. The surface layer of the steel absorbs carbon which hardens it. This process produces colours on the hardened parts of beautiful shades of blue and brown.

**Chamber** That part of the barrel breech end into which the cartridge is inserted.

**Choke** A constriction at the muzzle end of the barrel which should produce tighter patterns than if the barrel is bored cylinder. The amount of constriction or choke is measured in thousandths of an inch and termed 'points of choke'.

5 thous: would be 5 points of choke and termed Improved Cylinder.

10 thous: would be termed $\frac{1}{4}$ choke.

20 thous: would be termed $\frac{1}{2}$ choke or American modified choke.

30 thous: would be termed $\frac{3}{4}$ choke or American Improved modified choke.

40 thous: would be termed Full choke, or American full choke.

In practice such measurements bear little relation to the tightness and, more important, to the quality of the patterns thrown. Only by shooting cartridges can the layman ascertain the pattern spread and quality. Some imported guns with 40 thous constriction are overchoked, so much so that pellets are deformed by passing through such a tight choke. The resulting patterns are poor and patchy. A skilled barrel borer can often improve and tighten such patterns by opening the choke constriction. One can only repeat that it takes patterning and testing to obtain the true story. Experience from the last half century has satisfied me that pattern density and quality is not necessarily proportional to either the degree of constriction, or choke shape.

**Choke tubes** Screw-in, screw-on, drop-in tubes which are of varying constriction and which can alter the tightness of the pattern thrown by a barrel. Correctly used and maintained they increase the versatility of a gun.

**Chokes, recess** Where a gun is bored with little constriction and where there is sufficient thickness of metal at the muzzle end, it is sometimes possible for a skilled gunsmith to bore the barrel recess choke. About $\frac{1}{4}$ choke is the maximum that can be achieved.

**Chokes, retro or trumpet** Very similar to the Cutts compensator choke system. The barrel is expanded some 4 in from the muzzle and then swaged in again about $\frac{1}{2}$ in from the muzzle. This is alleged to separate the shot charge from felt or fibre driving wads. Also some of the shot pellets are distorted from the spherical thereby producing a longer shot string. This has been proved by Brister in his experiments.

**Cutts compensator chokes** Invented by Col. Cutts of the United States of America shortly after World War One. The compensator started life as a muzzle brake, slots being cut into the top of the compensator to reduce the tendency of the gun muzzle to climb when the gun was fired. The Lyman Gun Sight Co. applied the Cutts compensator to shotguns. There is no doubt that the slots do reduce recoil, also that various choke tubes can be screwed on the end to allow the shooter a choice of chokes. Compensators are not allowed for the going-away disciplines, such as DTL, but are allowed for Skeet and Sporting.

**Discipline** A word used for various types of clay competition shooting.

**DTL** Down the Line discipline.

**Ejectors** Pieces of mechanism which throw out the fired empty cases when a gun is opened.

**Engraving** A pattern cut into metal to make it more pleasing to those shooters with artistic tendencies.

**Extractors** Pieces of mechanism which partially lift either fired cases or unfired cartridges far enough out of the barrel chambers when the gun is opened to allow them to be taken out by hand.

**File cut** *See* **Ribs**

**FN Fabrique Nationale.** An old and famous firm of gunmakers in Liege, Belgium.

**Firing pin** *See* **Striker**

**Firing point, shooting stand, peg** A position marked on the ground, usually as a square with sides measuring 1 yd or 1 m. The shooter must stand with both feet inside this square when firing his gun.

FITASC Federation Internationale de Tir aux Armes Sportives de Chasse.

**Fore-end** A piece of wood placed in front of the action and under and/or partially around the barrel(s). The fore-end iron is fitted into this wood in the case of single barrel, side by sides, or o/us. With semi-automatics and pump guns the fore-end contains the magazine tube and extraction parts. On single barrel, or side by sides the wood may be of splinter or beavertail shape. On o/us it may be of Sporting/snable, schnozzle, or beavertail shape. On semi-automatics and pumps the fore-end shape is more rounded than true beavertail.

**Gauge** *See* **Bore/gauge**

**Gun canting** Due to many causes. The most usual being an ill-fitted butt with a long toe; to prevent this toe digging in the gun is canted to allow the toe to lie near the armpit.

**Guns** *O/U Over and Under.* The barrels are placed one on top of the other. American 'superposed'. This provides a narrow sighting plane which some shooters believe assists one seeing the target and more precise pointing of the gun. *Percussion* A muzzle-loading gun whose charge is fired by a percussion cap. *Pump* Single-barrelled magazine guns operated each time after firing by the shooter pumping or tromboning the fore-end backwards and forwards. As supplied by the makers is capable of being fired by an expert as quickly as a semi-automatic gun. For clay shooting only one cartridge is allowed to be placed in the magazine. Popular with rough shooters and wildfowlers. *SA* Single-barrelled semi-automatic magazine guns which are self-loading. Pulling the trigger should fire the gun, recoil or gas pressure moves the bolt rearward and ejects the empty case, the next cartridge is then fed up from the magazine into the barrel chamber and the bolt closes, leaving the gun ready to fire the second shot. The rules for some disciplines state that the magazine must be plugged to prevent the insertion of more than one cartridge. Popular with rough shooters or wildfowlers, but not for game shooting. It is difficult for the onlooker to know when these guns are unloaded, although the Bradley breech blocker does do this well. *SB* Single-shot, single-barrelled guns. Very popular in the USA for Trapshooting, rarely seen in this country. *S/S* The barrels are placed side by side, not so popular these days for targets. Still the number one choice for formal game shooting. To see a trained gun and loader handling and shooting a pair of 'best' guns is an education to the layman.

**Gun position** Out of the shoulder pocket as applied to FITASC sporting is now well defined and the gun butt position is now higher and closely under and touching the shoulder pocket.

**Gun position 'down'** A term used in ISU Skeet, the gun position for which is rigidly defined. This 'down' position has to be adopted before calling for the target(s) and held until the target(s) appear in view.

**Gun position 'optional'** A term used for ABT, American Skeet, DTL, OT, UT, English Sporting. The shooter can please himself whether or not he premounts his gun before calling for the target.

   Gun positions for live shooting are many, almost anything goes as long as the gun handling means the muzzles are pointed safely at all times.

**Hammer/tumbler** The part of the gun which hits the striker and eventually fires the cartridge. Most modern guns have hammers sited inside the action.

**Hammerless** A gun in which the hammers are unseen and inside the action.

**Hinge pin** The pin on which the barrels hinge when the gun is opened.

**Hinge pins/bifurcated** *See* **Bifurcated**

**ISU** International Shooting Union.

**Jointing** The hinge or joint of the barrels to the action.

**Kill** The referee's decision which cannot be overruled on whether or not the shooter has 'killed' his target.

**Lock** The moving parts of the action, cocking levers or dogs, springs, sears, tumblers, etc.

**Locks,** box *See* **Boxlock**

**Locks,** side *See* **Sidelock**

**'Locked up'** When gun and shooter are swinging as one unit, butt in shoulder pocket and cheek tight to stock comb.

**Lump** A protrusion underneath or on the sides of the barrels into which the locking bolts engage to hold barrel and action together.

**Magazine** Usually a tube under the barrel on semi-automatic or pump guns in which extra cartridges are held. For clay shooting the rules state a gun must not be loaded with more than two cartridges in total, regardless of magazine capacity. For live shooting the rules are in the melting pot until a new firearms bill is passed. Most magazine gun users have their magazines plugged to restrict the capacity to either one or two cartridges even now.

**Miss and out/sudden death** In tie shoots, where as soon as a shooter drops or misses a target he is out of the competition.

**Mono block** The barrel lumps are machined from a billet or block of steel and bored with two holes into which the barrels are inserted. They are usually soldered in place.

**Monte Carlo** A shape of stock comb usually parallel to the barrel top line for most of its length. Was originally used at Monte Carlo for guns used to shoot live pigeons. Such a correctly fitted gun and stock when properly mounted ensures that the shooter's aiming eye is always positioned at the same level in relation to the barrel rib, regardless where along the comb line his cheek is placed.

**Mono wads** *See* **Wads**

**OT** Olympic Trap or Trench.

**Over draft** A tendency for the barrels and action to partially close themselves after being opened. This is usually due to faulty design or poorly fitted cocking mechanism. Makes loading difficult. The ownership of such a gun should not be tolerated, it should not be bought.

**Over run** *See* **Over draft**

**Overshot wad** *See* **Wads**

**Patterns** The number in which pellets are distributed when fired from a gun onto a sheet of paper or a pattern plate. To obtain a reasonable estimate of pattern spread and quality a string of nine shots should be separately fired to evaluate one barrel and one type of cartridge. Should always be done with the gun fired at an accurately measured distance from the plate.

**Peg** *See* **Firing point**

**Percussion** *See* **Guns, percussion**

**Powder charge** The amount of powder used in a single cartridge. These charges are usually 'thrown' by volume. It is essential that home loaders check the amount of powder they are throwing by means of an accurate powder scale. Different batches of the same powder, if measured by volume, may vary in the weight of powder thrown by the same powder bush.

**Rail, running** A strip of rubber or similar, in a metal channel fixed to the trailing edge of a trap arm. The target runs along this, thereby acquiring spin when the arm is released.

**Recoil** The blow or push which a gun, when fired, gives the shooter. Based on the physics principle of 'no action without reaction'. W.W. Greener's formula postulated gun weight should be 96 times that of the shot charge to avoid excessive recoil. A 6 lb. gun would therefore use a 1 oz. shot load. Still holds good today for safe guns with correct head space and chamber length and which are loaded with suitable cartridges.

**Recoil pad** A rubber pad on the end of the stock. May be solid, or ventilated to soften the gun recoil on the shoulder.

**Ribs** Metal strips brazed, pegged or soldered on to barrels.

**Ribs, bottom** Placed below and slightly between the barrels of a side by side gun.

**Ribs, side** Placed each side and slightly between the barrels of an o/u gun.

**Ribs, top** May be floating, parallel, raised, solid, stepped, swamped, tapered or ventilated. With a selection of top surfaces such as cross-etched, cross-milled, file-cut, matted or smooth. Some, but not all shooters, find a top rib an aid in precise pointing of the gun.

**Safety catches** The safeties on most guns only block the movement of the trigger. They will not prevent sear noses being jarred out of bents. Catches may be automatic, in which case they are automatically returned to safe every time the gun is opened. Manual safety catches must be operated by the shooter as required.

**Sand bagger** One who by devious methods shoots in a lower class than his true form warrants. A difficult person against whom to legislate.

**Sear** The arm which holds the tumbler at full cock. Pressure on the sear by the trigger moves the sear nose out of bent, releases the tumbler, and fires the gun.

**Semi-automatic** *See* **Guns,** SA.

**Shoot-offs** If two or more shooters obtain equal scores in a competition, the first three places may be decided by shoot-off or tie shoot between the shooters concerned. May be shot off over a number of targets; alternatively, may be shot off as first miss and out, or sudden death.

**Shot string** The pellets of shot after being fired travel as a long column. The length of this column or string can vary immensely due to the components of the cartridge, the chokings and internal contours of the barrels.

**Shoulder pocket** The shoulder is brought forward slightly, thereby providing a hollow or pocket in which the gun butt is placed.

**Sidelock** A type of action similar to that used for hammer guns. The locks are mounted on the inside of the side plates with the hammers or tumblers also on the inside. (*See* illustrations on pages 23, 24 and 35.)

**Sights** *Centre* or *Intermediate*. A small metal or white bead fitted to the top rib about 15 in from the muzzle. *Front* The original front sight was a round bead of metal or ivory fitted on top of the rib near the muzzle. Now front sights are available in metal, ivory, plastic and other materials. They may be bead or toothpaste-shaped, plain, coloured or fluorescent.

**Silent rise** A term used in Sporting shooting. When the shooter says 'Ready' the target is released by non-visible or audible instruction from the referee. The delay before target release may be up to three seconds.

**Snap cap** A dummy cartridge, when placed in the barrel chamber allows the gun to be closed, and the trigger pulled with no damage to the firing pin or striker.

**Spread** The diameter of the shot pattern. Controlled mostly by the barrel choke. By shooting a gun at a pattern plate at known distances and measuring the spread diameter it is possible to assess the choking of the gun (*see* table 4 for the diameter of spread of shot pattern at various ranges).

**Squad hustler** An energetic gentleman whose job it is to encourage squads of shooters to be ready at the proper layout at the correct time. Rarely seen except in Britain, the onus is still on the shooter to be on any layout when required completely ready with gun and cartridges.

**Stock** Usually of wood, fitted behind the action at rear end of gun.

**Stock bolt** A large number of imported guns have stock and action held together by a stock bolt.

**Stock boot** A leather or rubber slip-over boot. Placed over the butt end of the stock to make it longer.

**Stock crawling** A habit common to trap shooters, the head is pushed out forward and down on the front end of the comb. This action puts extra tension on the neck muscles, the eyes have to be swivelled upwards to look out through the shooter's eyebrows. This encourages head lifting.

**Stock hand** That part of the stock held by the shooter's trigger hand. May be full pistol, half pistol or straight hand shaped.

**Stock head** The front part of the stock in front of the hand. This part is usually an extremely close fit into the back or rear of the action.

**Striker** Also known as the firing pin. This is the pin which strikes the cartridge cap. The majority of British side by side boxlocks have the striker pin integral with the hammer or tumbler. Imported guns usually have separate striker or firing pins.

**Stud bolt** Sometimes when cast is put into a stock the stock bolt will not then go through the stock. When this occurs a bent bolt is made with a screw-on nut. When the bolt is fixed into the back of the action the stock is pushed on and the nut screwed on the stud to hold all together.

**Swept out** Some shooters have the face of the stock comb swept out. Very often this results in the need for cast off being reduced or eliminated.

**Target ridden in** Allowing the muzzles to keep swinging with the target until it is so close that successful breaking may be dangerous and difficult.

**Target ridden out** The opposite to the above and just as conducive to missing.

**Thous:** Thousandths of an inch.

**Toe** The point at the bottom rear end of the stock.

**Top extension** A metal extension usually fitted to the barrel(s) at the breech.

**Top lever** A lever on the top of the action used to open the gun.

**Trigger** The part which the shooter pulls or presses to fire the gun. May be two on a double-barrelled gun, in which case the front trigger usually fires the right barrel on a side by side, and the bottom barrel on an o/u. Single triggers on double guns may be selective or non-selective.

**Trigger guard strap** A metal strip fixed to action and around the trigger(s) to prevent them catching on an obstruction and firing the gun.

**Trigger plate** The plate to which the trigger assembly is fitted. A trigger plate action is one where most of the striker mechanism is fitted to the plate and may be removed as a unit.

**Trigger pulls** The amount of pull or pressure, usually measured in pounds and ounces, required to be exerted on the trigger to take the sear out of bent and fire the gun.

**Tromboning** Sliding the hand back along the barrels during the swing. Was popular years ago amongst those who specialized in driven game shooting and who first mounted their guns with a long front hand, as they swung along the line of the incoming bird the front hand was slid backwards down the barrels to prevent the swing of the gun being blocked.

**Tubes** Barrels begin life as blanks, becoming tubes after boring, becoming barrels after they have been joined together, had loops, lumps and ribs fitted, and been chambered, rimmed and finally fine bored and regulated.

**Tumblers** *See* **Hammer/tumbler**

**Tune** A term used for setting trigger pulls. A skilled operation for an expert, who will tune pulls to be short, crisp, and take the sear nose out of bent at the precise poundage specified by the customer.

**UT** Universal or Five Trap Trench.

**Ventilated rib** *See* **Ribs**

**Wads** Used in cartridges to separate powder and shot; acts also as a piston when the cartridge is fired and the shot propelled up and out of the barrels. *Card* Used over the powder and/or under the shot, originally the over powder card wad was used to prevent grease from the felt wads from contaminating the powder. Under shot wads were used to prevent the bottom layer of pellets sticking to the greased felt wad. *Felt* Made of wool felt and sandwiched between the over powder and under shot card wads, the felt wad is rarely used these days. *Kleena* A vegetable fibre wad used by Eley as the main driving wad for some of their cartridges. *Mono* A plastic one-piece wad consisting of over powder cup, connecting collapsible legs and shot cup. Used by Eley in some of its clay target cartridges. *Plaswad* A British-made plastic wad highly popular with the home loader. *Various* Makers of modern cartridges such as Game Bore, Fiocchi, Hull Cartridge, Maionchi, Remington, SMI, Winchester and others have their own specially designed plastic wads to suit their particular caps, cases, powder, etc. In addition, most of them also use sophisticated combination wads made of cork, fibre, plastic and other materials, to produce cartridges of high and consistent performance. There are also special wads which will help to produce a wider pattern than normal from a tightly choked barrel; these are called spreader wads and cartridges so wadded are named spreader or dispersante cartridges.

**WAGBI** *See* BASC

**White line spacers** White washers of plastic used to fit between recoil pad and butt end to lengthen stock and in some shooters' opinions, embellish it.

# Index